# Copyrights

# TABLE of CONTENTS

# Political Insight

This is my political insight Message We live in a political world marked by deep polarization, where the line between truth and misinformation is increasingly blurred. Global challenges such as climate change, economic inequality, and the rise of authoritarianism test the resilience of democratic institutions. Amidst these complexities, the right to vote—a cornerstone of democracy—is increasingly under threat. In many regions, efforts to strip away voting rights or implement restrictive laws have made it harder for citizens, especially marginalized communities, to exercise their fundamental rights. Voter suppression tactics, gerrymandering, and disinformation campaigns undermine the democratic process, eroding trust in the very systems meant to uphold it. Yet, despite these barriers, there is a growing movement of citizens who are more engaged and vocal, demanding transparency, accountability, and meaningful change from their leaders. The political landscape is in constant flux, shaped by a tug-of-war between progress and regression, making it more crucial than ever to stay informed, protect voting rights, and critically assess the forces shaping our future.

Written By: Dr.Alice Teague Author of Spotlight Spectacular Magazine.

# Dr. Alice Teague

Dr. Alice Yancy Teague is a stalwart in forensic pathology, and a relentless advocate for criminal justice reform. Recognized nationwide for her unwavering commitment to excellence, Dr. Alice is a beacon of inspiration, transcending boundaries with her expertise and passion. Armed with a distinguished Academic background including being a Pre-Med Student at the age of 25 years under the regional Hats Adam program: Chicago, Illinois.

She was a nurse, a physical assistant, grandfather in as a pathologist in forensic science since 2008. Dr. Alice has a B.S. in Criminal Justice and a Masters in Public Administration. She has garnered acclaim, earning prestigious certifications such as:

- Certified Court Mediator
- Certified FEMA Federal Emergency Management certification
- Certified Leadership Influence and Management System (NIMS)
- Certified Megan Speaker (Fix My Credit) through the Maxwell Institute
- Certified in Community Civil Training Covington Ga. (Police Academy), and more.

She has also won prestigious award titles such as:

- Woman of the Year Awards, 2005, held in Chicago, Illinois
- The revered Cambridge Who's Who Registry 2007-2008 Edition, Chicago Illinois
- She has participated in the Walk of Hope Breast Cancer 2019
- Women of Empowerment, Honorary 2019
- Women over 40 competition, in which she received 2nd place recognition.

Kimberley Chance Atkin Breast cancer foundation 2019 honoree award for the wall of hope.

She was once a member of the Rainbow Push Coalition and the 4th Congressional Federation of Democratic women. She is also the founder of Women of Color Breast Cancer Organization; as well as the founder of Break Every Chain Re-entry Program for Returning Citizens. As a visionary entrepreneur, Dr. Alice has left an indelible mark through ventures like Family Health Care Inc., Elisa South Food restaurant, Elisa Creation clothing store, Legal Resource services, Bounce House Creation. She also hosts the Dr. Alice Show Atlanta TV 1061, Youtube and Roku channels and is the author of Spotlight Spectacular Magazine.

Her literary prowess is demonstrated through her groundbreaking book "You are What you Eat", first published by Author House in June 2010. Another example is her forthcoming 2nd Book , set for release in October 2024, titled "Pink Ribbon". Beyond her professional endeavors, Dr. Alice has boldly ventured into politics as a two-time Presidential Candidate of the United States, reflecting her unwavering dedication to driving transformation on a grand scale.

Dr. Alice was originally born in Chicago, Illinois, but relocated to Georgia in 2010. She is a mother of two adult children and a grandmother of three. She also prides herself on being a member of the Stonecrest Church of Christ McDonough Ga., where Dr. Richard Barclay senior minister located at 750 Mount Carmel Road, McDonough, Georgia 30253

# WELCOME TO AUGUST

# EMBRACE THE GOLDEN GOODBYES

Where every day is a golden opportunity to shine. In this special month, the sun lingers a little longer, casting a warm, golden hue over everything it touches. August is a month of transition, where summer's exuberance begins to mellow, preparing to hand over its reign to the gentle whispers of autumn.

As the days stretch lazily, there's a unique charm in the air, an invitation to savor each moment before the seasons change .
August is a month of endless possibilities and quiet reflections. It's the perfect time to soak up the last rays of summer sun, to let the warmth sink into your soul, and to create memories that will carry you through the cooler months ahead.

Whether it's a final beach getaway, a backyard barbecue with friends and family, or simply a peaceful evening watching the sunset, August encourages us to embrace the beauty of the present moment.

So, as we journey through this golden month, let us celebrate the vibrant tapestry of experiences it offers. Let us revel in the laughter of children playing in the park, the sweet taste of fresh summer fruits, and the serene stillness of a warm evening. August reminds us that life is a series of fleeting moments, each one precious and worth cherishing.

As you turn the pages of this edition, we hope you find inspiration in the stories of those who shine brightly, just like the August sun. Let their tales remind you to make the most of every moment, to find joy in the simple pleasures, and to embrace the golden goodbye of summer with open arms.

Author : Dr. Alice Teague C.E.O. of Spotlight Spectacular Magazine

      We see You

# DR RICHARD LEE BARCLAY
## From The State Of Georgia

When he was only eight years ago, Richard Lee Barclay knew he wanted to preach. At age 12, he was assistant superintendent for the Pleasant Hill Baptist Church in Woodville, Texas Sunday school, and he began preaching at the age of 16 at the church. Having completed high school, he enrolled at East Texas Baptist University in Marshall, having been awarded an academic scholarship by the Southern Baptist General Convention of Texas.

His plan was to become a Baptist minister. God's plan was that at age 20 the brass young man, over confident with some new knowledge he had acquired in some of his classes at ETBU, went to Westside Church of Christ in Marshall to "straighten out" the minister, W.F. Washington on some things he heard him preach—he got straightened out and was baptized into the Lord's church! At age 21, he began as a Church of Christ preacher in Smithland, a small community near Jefferson, Texas. This marked the beginning of his illustrious career as one of the preeminent ministers in Churches of Christ

A native of Woodville, Texas, Richard Barclay was born February 16, 1952. He graduated from Woodville High School, with honors in 1970; and, in 1975, he graduated from East Texas Baptist University in Marshall, Texas with a bachelor's degree with a major in sociology and a minor in religion. Always seeking to improve himself through formal education, he studied at Sunset School of Preaching in Lubbock, Texas in 1976 and continued this graduate work in 1980 at Boston University, Boston, Massachusetts.

Richard earned a master's degree from Gordon Conwell Theological Seminary in Boston, Massachusetts in 1983, and he did graduate work at George Pepperdine University in Malibu, California in 1986. He earned a second master's degree in theology in 1990 from the California Graduate School of Theology in Anaheim, California.

He was enrolled in a doctoral program in theology from 1990-1991 at California Graduate School of Theology in Anaheim, California. Barclay has been the evangelist to the Hillcrest Church of Christ in Corpus Christi, Texas (19771979); the Roxbury Church of Christ in Boston, Massachusetts (1979-1984); The Compton Avenue Church of Christ in Los Angeles, California (1984-1991); and the East Cotton Street Church of Christ in Longview, Texas (1991-1995). He served as the evangelist for the Kashmere Gardens Church of Christ in Houston, Texas from 1995 to 2006.

The former senior minister of the Hillcrest Church of Christ in Decatur, Georgia (2006-2017), he led the congregation in a multi-million dollar building additions and renovations. Leading up to the building program, the dynamic minister launched Operation

NOTE (New Opportunities To Expand), a capital stewardship campaign to liquidate the church's mortgage. He organized BRICK (Building Resources by Increasing Commitment to the Kingdom), another capital stewardship campaign during which more than $2 million was raised for the construction of a new auditorium and administrative wing.

Too, he initiated a number of innovative ministries including golf and theatre arts. Also, he was editor-in-chief of the church newsletter, The Hillcrest Herald. Also, while he was minister at the Hillcrest congregation, he co-hosted the 70h Annual Churches of Christ National Lectureship. In addition, at Hillcrest, he organized Remembrance Sunday, a day to celebrate the lives of those who have transitioned. During his tenure with the Hillcrest Church, the Decatur, Georgia branch of the NAACP recognized him as outstanding pastor in the community. An avid golfer, he enjoys time on the links—a welcomed break from his demanding schedule; during his time at the Hillcrest Church, he organized an invitational golf tournament that raised money for a scholarship fund. Too, his desire to share the sport with Hillcrest youth led to the formation of a youth golf camp. He recently answered a call from God to plant a church and is currently growing the Stonecrest Church of Christ in Lithonia, Georgia, with indications of a successful endeavor demonstrated by an initial gathering of some 250 Christians.

He has led to Stonecrest Church to purchase a 45,000 square foot facility located on 12 acres of land in McDonough, Georgia where more than 350 assembled for their opening in October, 2018. Richard is a nationally known expositor of God's word and has preached and conducted meetings in over 40 states. He was privileged to preach in South Africa and Ethiopia in 1989 and 1994. He is a much sought-after speaker who has spoken at several lectureships and seminars including: Texas State Lectureship, Northeastern Lectureship (keynote address), Florida Evangelism Seminar (keynote address), Southwestern Christian College Lectureship, Abilene Christian University, Pepperdine University in Malibu, California; Houston City-wide Lectureship, Northeastern Youth Conference (keynote address), New England Evangelism Seminar, the National Church Lectureship (keynote addresses), and David Lipscomb University Lectureship (keynote address).

He conducted a very popular radio ministry, "Let The Bible Speak," in Boston, Massachusetts and conducted a television program "Sonshine From Heaven" for the Kashmere Gardens Church of Christ in Houston, Texas. Barclay served as the publicity chairman for the Los Angeles Campaign for Christ which was an annual cooperative effort held in August.  A skilled writer, Richard served as a staff writer for the following publications: "Restoration Pulpit," "Watts Times," "Gospel Advocate" and "20th Century Christian."

He continues to write for the "Christian Echo," and he was the founding editor of two magazines: "Manna," a family oriented magazine published bi-monthly and "Kerusso," a quarterly publication designed for serious Bible students. He has published two books, Where Your Treasure Is… and Marriage by Design. Community involvement has been important to Barclay. During his tenure in Longview at the East Cotton congregation, he served on the Longview Branch NAACP Religious Affairs Committee as the chairman, the Gregg County Airport Board, the Board of Directors for the East Texas Literacy Council and the Longview Independent School District Public Information Advisory Committee. He served as the chaplain for the Longview Police Department and worked with the City of Longview Drug Task Force.

Additionally, Richard worked with the Texas Adolescent and Family Substance Abuse Academy as well as, the South Longview Economic Development Council. In Houston, he was honored to be the commencement speaker for Kashmere Gardens High School. He has developed a number of ministries at the Kashmere Gardens congregation, including prison, the Sunshine, Singles, seasoned saints, FLOCKS, couples, men's, African American history, and youth. He also initiated Founder's Day and the Family Night program.

He was editor-in-chief of the church's newsletter, The Garden and, he hosted the National Singles Conference in Houston. Recognizing the importance of being active in the community, he served on the Board of Trustees for The Miracle Corporation.

Additionally, he was on the board of The Urban League and Julia C. Hester House; and he was a consultant for Continuum Healthcare. Also, while he was in Houston, Barclay was instrumental in helping to bridge the racial divide longstanding in religious academia, serving on the Racial Reconciliation Committee at Abilene Christian University; he taught hermeneutics at the Houston Christian Institute.

Recognized throughout the brotherhood for his powerful series on stewardship, he has also conducted numerous, highly touted seminars on marriage. He was recently named director of the Southwestern Christian College Lectureship held annually in Terrell, Texas. Southwestern also conferred on Barclay its honorary Doctorate of Humane Letter degree at its Spring graduation where Dr. Barclay was its commencement speaker. Dr. Barclay was recently appointed to the Board of Directors of The Solomon Foundation, a church extension fund that finances churches associated with the Restoration Movement. He now serves as secretary of the Board.

Richard is married to Shirley Brooks Barclay, a retired educator; the couple has two adult sons, Christopher, a computer programmer for Verizon, and Reginald, a successful Houston businessman

# *Contribution*



## OR TOTAL COMMITMENT

You may have heard the story of the chicken and the pig. They were walking down the street one day and came to a grocery store. There was a sign in the window that said, "Bacon and eggs needed." The chicken looked at the pig and said, "Let's help the grocer out." The pig responded: "You must be crazy. For you that's just a contribution, but for me that's a total commitment!"

That's how a lot of men feel about the Christian life. "Hey, I don't mind contributing a little here and there. But let's not go overboard. Let's not get into this total commitment thing." That sounds a little too scary for a lot of guys, as if the Christian life is going to cost them too much. So, they give a part of themselves to Christ, but hold back the rest in case the Christian life gets too demanding.

In my small East Texas town of Woodville, where I grew up, they call that "jiving and half-stepping." That's when you try to walk with Christ and walk with the world at the same time. You might call it "two-timing." The Bible calls it double mindedness (James 1:8). Whatever you call it, it's what happens when you try to love Christ and love the world at the same time. But love doesn't work that way. It always calls for commitment. In this article, I want to call you past the excuses people make and show you the excitement, the spiritual power, and the overflowing joy that await the person who is committed, sold out, to Jesus Christ. 5 The Anatomy of Commitment

In Romans 12:1–2, Paul gives what I call the anatomy of commitment: I appeal to you therefore, brothers, by the mercies of God, to present your bodies as a living sacrifice, holy and acceptable to God, which is your spiritual worship. Do not be conformed to this world, but be transformed by the renewal of your mind, that by testing you may discern what is the will of God, what is good and acceptable and perfect

Since everything we do is expressed through our bodies, Paul calls us to present our bodies as living sacrifices to God. The concept of a living sacrifice is interesting because it sounds like a contradiction. In the Mosaic system, a sacrifice was killed. Yet Paul wants us to remain alive. We are literally to be walking dead people. How is this possible? Paul's understanding of his own life helps us here.

He says: "I have been crucified with Christ. It is no longer I who live, but Christ who lives in me" (Gal. 2:20). If you were to ask Paul what his goals in life were, he probably would say: "I don't have any. Dead people don't set goals." If you could ask him what his dreams were, he would respond, "Dead people don't dream." But if you were to ask him what God's goals and dreams for him were, no doubt he could talk all day long, because even though Paul was dead to himself, he was alive to God.

GOD'S GOALS HAD BECOME PAUL'S GOALS. GOD'S DESIRES HAD BECOME PAUL'S DESIRES. THE ONLY LIFE HE HAD WAS THE LIFE OF CHRIST. THIS IS WHY NO ONE COULD INTIMIDATE THIS MAN.

IF HIS ENEMIES THREATENED TO KILL HIM, HE COULD SAY, "TO DIE IS GAIN" (PHIL. 1:21B). IF THEY SAID, "NO, WE'RE GOING TO LET YOU LIVE," HE COULD ANSWER: "THAT'S FINE. 'TO LIVE IS CHRIST'" (1:21A). IF THEY SAID, "WE'RE GOING TO BEAT YOU," HE COULD SAY, "I CONSIDER THAT THE SUFFERINGS OF THIS PRESENT TIME ARE NOT WORTH COMPARING WITH THE GLORY THAT IS TO BE REVEALED TO US" (ROM. 8:18).
IF PAUL DIED, HE WOULD GO TO BE WITH CHRIST. IF HE LIVED, HE WOULD SERVE CHRIST. AND IF HE SUFFERED, HE WOULD GET MORE REWARD FROM CHRIST

THEREFORE, SINCE HIS WHOLE LIFE BELONGED TO CHRIST, PAUL'S ATTITUDE WAS THAT IT REALLY DID NOT MATTER WHAT HAPPENED TO HIM.

THIS KIND OF COMMITMENT IS SO IMPORTANT THAT PAUL CALLS IT OUR "SPIRITUAL ACT OF WORSHIP." NOTICE THAT PAUL DOESN'T SAY, "IF YOU WANT TO BE COMMITTED, GO TO CHURCH." WORSHIP STARTS WITH THE COMMITMENT OF OUR LIVES, NOT WITH OUR CHURCH ATTENDANCE. WE SHOULD GO TO CHURCH TO DO CORPORATELY ON A WEEKLY BASIS WHAT WE ARE ALREADY DOING INDIVIDUALLY ON A DAILY BASIS. IT'S TRAGIC THAT SO MANY PEOPLE WORSHIP GOD ON SUNDAY BUT IGNORE HIM —OR EVEN WORSE, WORSHIP THEMSELVES—THE REST OF THE WEEK. WHEN YOU'RE A LIVING SACRIFICE, EVERY ACTIVITY OF YOUR LIFE BECOMES AN ACT OF WORSHIP.

# THE MOTIVATION FOR COMMITMENT

Look at the reason Paul gives as to why we should present our bodies as living sacrifices to God. It's because of "God's mercy."

Now, there's so much packed into that term that it would take the rest of this article to develop it fully. Basically, "God's mercy" refers to all that has gone before in the first eleven chapters of Romans. Let me summarize what this means for you and me as Christians today. The first three chapters of Romans explain that the whole world, you and I included, is guilty before God. "None is righteous, no, not one" (Rom. 3:10). This is the bad news. But then, in the second half of Romans 3, Paul gives us the good news of Jesus's sacrifice on the cross that brought humankind into a right relationship with God. We were justified or declared righteous before God because Christ's blood satisfied the demands of a holy God against sinful men (3:21–26)

Then, in the fourth chapter of Romans, Paul explains that salvation is granted to us in response to faith, not works. This means that our salvation is free and cannot be gained through any human merit. Rather, God gives it away to undeserving sinners. That is mercy. When we do present our bodies to God, we can be assured of victory, as the eighth chapter of Romans shows. God has given us the indwelling Holy Spirit, who empowers us to experience all the rights and privileges God has for his children. This power is awesome, assuring us that "we know that for those who love God all things work together for good, for those who are called according to his purpose" (Rom. 8:28). In a nutshell, those are the mercies of God to you and me. They deserve only one kind of response—the response of total commitment

# Rejecting Worldliness

In Romans 12:2, Paul expands on what it means to commit ourselves to God. "Do not be conformed to this world, but be transformed by the renewal of your mind, that by testing you may discern what is the will of God, what is good and acceptable and perfect." He tells us that as Christians, we are not to let the world order define who we are. Total commitment includes rejecting the attempts of this satanically controlled world system to get us to exclude God from our lives. The essence of worldliness is independence from God. On a constant and unrelenting basis, the world order seeks to convince you and me to leave God out of our lives

## A Transformed Mind

Being worldly doesn't mean only committing gross sins. Neither does it mean going to so-called worldly places. The heart of worldliness is simply leaving God out, excluding his rulership from our daily lives. Neither do you have to kill anybody or commit immorality to be worldly. All you have to do is let the world conform you to its shape, the way a potter forms a lump of clay into a bowl or pitcher. Rejecting that pressure is impossible unless you are committed without reservation to Jesus Christ. A mushy, "half-stepping" kind of Christian life won't get the job done

Why does God want our minds? Because that is where the decisions of life are made. If we are going to be committed to Christ, He must have control of our minds. The word transformed in Romans 12:2 is passive. In other words, the transforming work is done by someone other than us. If we commit ourselves to God and reject the world, the Holy Spirit takes over and begins the renewal and growth process. The implications of this are staggering, as we will now see.

## **You Won't Produce unless You Grow**

If you are a committed Christian, you are a growing Christian. Growth follows commitment like day follows night.

Spiritual growth is possible because the Christian life is a dynamic, living thing. That's why Jesus used the analogy of a vineyard to deliver one of his most important messages on the process of spiritual growth: I am the true vine, and my Father is the vinedresser. Every branch in me that does not bear fruit he takes away, and every branch that does bear fruit he prunes, that it may bear more fruit. Already you are clean because of the word that I have spoken to you.

Abide in me, and I in you. As the branch cannot bear fruit by itself, unless it abides in the vine, neither can you, unless you abide in me. I am the vine; you are the branches. Whoever abides in me and I in him, he it is that bears much fruit, for apart from me you can do nothing. If anyone does not abide in me he is thrown away like a branch and withers; and the branches are gathered, thrown into the fire, and burned. If you abide in me, and my words abide in you, ask whatever you wish, and it will be done for you. By this my Father is glorified, that you bear much fruit and so prove to be my disciples. As the Father has loved me, so have I loved you. Abide in my love. If you keep my commandments, you will abide in my love, just as I have kept my Father's commandments and abide in his love. These things I have spoken to you, that my joy may be in you, and that your joy may be full. (John 15:1–11)

When Jesus refers to a branch that is "in me," he is not talking about those who are merely acquainted with him. He is referring to people who are in a vital, personal relationship with him. But some of these branches do not bear fruit, so the Father "takes [them] away" (John 15:2). The Greek verb used here can also be translated as "lifts [them] up." In grape growing, branches sometimes droop too close to the ground and become covered in dust. They fail to get the sunlight they need and begin to wither.

The vinedresser lifts these branches off the ground and brushes off the accumulated dust, making sure they get the life-giving light they need. Then, if possible, he ties these branches to poles or posts to keep them from drooping to the ground. In other words, the vinedresser gives nonproductive branches every opportunity to produce fruit. How does God "lift up" his people? He does so through encouragement, for one thing. I've seen it again and again, especially with new Christians, who haven't had time to grow their branches very far from the ground. I've seen God answer prayers that seemed impossible. I've seen him make a way out of an inescapable situation. I've seen him solve problems that appeared insurmountable.

All the person on the receiving end could say was, "Thank you, Jesus!" His praise was the beginning of fruit-bearing, the continuous offer to God of "a sacrifice of praise" (Heb. 13:15).

## The Pruning Process: Short-Term Pain for Long-Term Gain

Going from producing no fruit to producing some fruit is an important step. But it's still just the beginning. Once you become committed to Christ and start reflecting a Christian character, God prunes your branches to help you produce more fruit. Pruning is the process of trimming off unwanted shoots that can rob the branches of the nourishment they would otherwise receive from the vine. In grape growing, these are called "sucker shoots," little branches that grow where the vine and branch intersect. As they grow larger, they begin to do exactly what their name suggests— they suck away the life-giving sap on its way from the vine to the branch. In John 15:3, Jesus reminds us that we have been made clean, or saved, by the Word he has spoken to us. Just as we are saved by hearing and trusting the Word of Christ (Romans 10:17; Acts 2:37-38), we are also kept clean by hearing and heeding that same Word. That's why it is critical for us to maintain regular exposure to the Bible, which is God's fixed revelation to us. As the psalmist said, "I have stored up your word in my heart, that I might not sin against you" (Ps. 119:11). The Word of God is our spiritual cleansing agent, purging out the undesirable junk—the sucker shoots—that collects in our lives so that we can become fruitful for Christ.

# THE CLEANSING POWER OF GOD'S WORD

## THE SECRET TO YOUR SPIRITUAL SUCCESS

The real secret to growth and fruitfulness in your spiritual life is remaining in Christ (John 15:4). The word abide means "to stay or remain." It's what happens when you put a tea bag in a cup of hot water. As the tea bag "abides" or remains in the water, it influences the water so that the water begins to reflect the color and taste of the tea. Of course, the longer the bag abides in the water, the stronger the tea. This is exactly what happens when you abide in Christ and he abides in you. The influence of Christ so pervades your life that you begin to reflect the character and nature of your Lord. Now, the beauty of abiding is that all we have to do is maintain our contact with Christ to have the desired result.

A tea bag really doesn't have any excuse not to produce results once it is dipped into the cup. In fact, it doesn't need any excuse, as long as it stays put. The trouble with many of us is that we are not good "abiders." We think we can survive apart from the vine. We provide for our families, so why ask God for our daily bread? We work, so why depend on someone else, even God, for our needs? You and I may work and do a lot of other things, but according to Jesus, we can do "nothing" without him (John 15:5). Now, you may say: "Wait a minute, Dr. Barclay. Is that really true? Didn't you just mention some of the things we can do?" Sure, there's a lot we can do without Christ.

But taken as a whole, it amounts to nothing. Jesus is saying that without his indwelling presence, we can do nothing that's pleasing or acceptable to God. We can do nothing to further our spiritual growth without Christ.

In John 15:7–8, Jesus gives us the flip side of the coin. Going it alone results in fiery trials. But abiding has incredible benefits. "If you abide in me, and my words abide in you, ask whatever you wish, and it will be done for you. By this my Father is glorified, that you bear much fruit and so prove to be my disciples."

### An Open-Ended Offer

I know this promise is often quoted by unscrupulous and unscriptural preachers on religious television. But they don't give you the whole picture. Jesus did not simply say, "Ask for anything." He said to abide, then ask. Our world is full of people who ask but don't abide. But I don't want to rob this promise of its power. Jesus can make such a promise to his abiders because he knows they will ask only for what pleases him, helps them bear "much fruit," and thus glorifies the Father. How does one know one is abiding in Christ?

The measuring rod is obedience (John 15:10). If you lack obedience to Christ's commands, forget about praying. If you are not obeying Christ, you might as well get up off your knees, unfold your hands, open your eyes, and go for a walk.

Jesus said that only those who abide in him can expect to receive what they ask for, and obedience is the key to abiding. But if you are vitally connected to Jesus Christ and completely committed to obeying his commands despite your flaws and failures, then don't hesitate to tell him what's on your heart. Why? Because what you want from him is identical to what he wants for you.

And while you're waiting for the answer, God gives you something to make the wait worthwhile: joy. "These things I have spoken to you, that my joy may be in you, and that your joy may be full" (John 15:11). Joy is different from happiness. Joy has nothing to do with how things are going. Instead, it has to do with a God-given, internal quality of life.

It can produce peace in the midst of panic, calm in the midst of chaos, and tranquility in the midst of turmoil. Therefore, for the committed Christian, spiritual growth is a process, just like growing grapes is a process. The fruit God wants to see in our lives is likeness to Christ, from which flow the good works that please God and demonstrate our faith to others

## The Importance of Faith

If we are going to stop "half-stepping" with Christ and move out in commitment, we need to know what that commitment involves. We need to understand the process by which we grow as Christians. And we need to grasp the importance of faith to the life of commitment. After all, Hebrews 11:6 says, "Without faith it is impossible to please [God]." It's safe to say that we cannot live powerfully on earth as Christians without a significant measure of faith. So I want to help you see how important it is that we learn to live by faith. To do this, I want to back up to Hebrews 11:1, which says, "Now faith is the assurance of things hoped for, the conviction of things not seen."

## Genuine Faith Follows Through

To believe in what you can see requires no faith; it's right there in front of you. But to be convinced that what you cannot see is real, and to have as much confidence in its reality as you do in what you can see, hear, taste, touch, and smell, is genuine faith.

But there's more to the word conviction than just a firm belief. It refers to a certainty that we are willing to act upon. In other words, we have to do more than talk about faith to actually have faith. I'm reminded of the story of a high-wire walker who amazed audiences from coast to coast around the beginning of the twentieth century. In what was billed as the biggest stunt in history, this daring young man stretched a wire from one side of Niagara Falls to the other. Then, as an enormous audience looked on, he walked casually back and forth across the wire. He followed this with another round trip, this time riding a unicycle. For his next feat, he pushed a wheelbarrow loaded with bricks across and back. After executing each of these tasks flawlessly and without even working up a sweat, he stood on the platform and addressed the crowd.

"Do you believe I can cross the falls on this wire with a loaded wheelbarrow?" he asked. Of course, the crowd applauded. They had just seen him do exactly that. "Do you believe I can push this wheelbarrow across the falls with a man riding in it?" Again, the crowd roared, eager to see him try. "Very well," he said, motioning to a gentleman in the front row who was clapping his hands furiously. "Get in." Before he even had a chance to stop clapping, that man discovered the difference between genuine faith and mere "mental assent"! Faith requires follow-through.

When I talk about faith in the context of Christian commitment, I'm talking about that quality of trust in and reliance on Christ through the power of the Holy Spirit that enables us to do what he has asked us to do. The book of James has several good examples of what I mean. In James 2:14, we learn that our faith must be demonstrated by our works. "What good is it, my brothers, if someone says he has faith but does not have works?" James is saying that the faith we are to exercise as Christians has to be more than just talk.

The illustration he uses in James 2:15–17 brings this out. If someone comes to you hungry and ill-clothed, he doesn't need just a pat on the back and the assurance that if he will just trust God, everything will be fine. He needs food and clothes. The point is that the benefits of faith do not happen to Christians just because they believe the right things, but rather because they execute the right actions based on that belief. If you are a defeated Christian today, it could be that you suffer from the problem many of James's readers suffered from: theology without practice, which James argues is useless to God. The issue James wants us to wrestle with is not whether we have faith. That's already been established. He is concerned about the usefulness of our faith.

When I talk about faith in the context of Christian commitment, I'm talking about that quality of trust in and reliance on Christ through the power of the Holy Spirit that enables us to do what he has asked us to do.

The book of James has several good examples of what I mean. In James 2:14, we learn that our faith must be demonstrated by our works. "What good is it, my brothers, if someone says he has faith but does not have works?" James is saying that the faith we are to exercise as Christians has to be more than just talk.

Dr. Richard L. Barclay
Atlanta, Georgia

The illustration he uses in James 2:15–17 brings this out. If someone comes to you hungry and ill-clothed, he doesn't need just a pat on the back and the assurance that if he will just trust God, everything will be fine. He needs food and clothes. The point is that the benefits of faith do not happen to Christians just because they believe the right things, but rather because they execute the right actions based on that belief. If you are a defeated Christian today, it could be that you suffer from the problem many of James's readers suffered from: theology without practice, which James argues is useless to God. The issue James wants us to wrestle with is not whether we have faith. That's already been established. He is concerned about the usefulness of our faith.

P NAACP
ACP
Founded 1909
d 1909
AAC
Founded 190

Dr. Richard Barclay, Stonecrest Church of Christ, 750 Mt, Caramel Rd, McDonough, GA, 30253

Carey B. Barnes is man of God who strives to do God's will. He currently serves as an Elder at Stonecrest Church of Christ, is married to Elizabeth Barnes. He served as Minister of Education for 6 years and taught Adult Bible class for approximately 4 years. In addition to teaching, he has been preaching the Gospel for over 17 years. He served as Counselor for the Church for over 5 years, as well as, an advisor to the Senior Minister.

Carey's secular education earned him a Master of Science in Sociology with minors in Criminal Justice. He completed courses in religious studies and attributes his extensive training in public and business speaking to Valdosta State University. His experience in speaking to large and small groups, conferences or meetings to the U.S. Army, and all accomplished through his walk with Christ.

The Ripple Effect of a Minister and His Family

First of all, let's look at the term ripple effect: a situation in which one thing causes a series of other things to happen. A college professor once said that dropping a penny in a pale of water will not only affect the pale of water but impact the entire world. Once the penny strikes the water, it enters with a small splash, but ripples of waves are
created from this one incident. From a world point of view, the penny is taken out of circulation appears to be so minute. However, it's one coin that has been taken out of circulation, impacts the coins minted, and is the first sign of a shortage. A shortage that more prevalent with more and more coins of this value or taken out of circulation around the world.

By the same notion, if we look at the impact or effect in relations to a minister and his family, isolated, it appears to be inconsequential. Therefore, we must look at factors that are common and prevalent in a majority of ministers and their families. Pastors and ministry leaders are on the front lines preaching, teaching, leading people to Christ and developing leaders for Kingdom impact throughout the world. They touch thousands—and ultimately through eternity, millions—of
people with the Good News. Their vision is to see healthy, transformed ministry leaders impacting the body of Christ with a powerful, eternal ripple effect.

Let's go back to the beginning – to Genesis. God creates man and woman in His image, thus establishing the dignity of every human being. But why create Eve? Why not just stop at Adam? God articulates an essential truth prior to his creation of Eve – "it is not good that the man should be alone" (Genesis 2:18). Here it is revealed that humans are social creatures in need of companionship and meaningful relationships. From Adam and Eve the covenant of marriage is established, and the fruit of that covenant is children – a family – the basic unit of the social fabric of society itself.

For better, or for worse, the family is that single penny being dropped in the pale of water. The family as an "institution" is prior to any recognition by public authority, which has an obligation to recognize it". In other words, the family must be recognized by societies and governments; all laws should work towards upholding the sanctity of the institution God has established from the beginning of time. When human laws and decisions fail to respect this fundamental truth, the Church and the whole world suffers. But when the dignity of the family is

upheld and protected, the ripple effects on the world can be profound – disciples are formed, vocations are born, Saints are raised.

There must be a call to Family, Community, and Participation. Throughout Scripture, the duty to love one's family is emphasized countless times. From Genesis, where we are told to be our brother and sister's keeper (Genesis 4:8-15), to Exodus when we are given the fifth commandment – to honor one's mother and father, to the holiness of Noah, Abraham & Sarah, Ruth, this theme is repeated. In the New Testament, these commandments are carried forth, but they are transformed. Your family, your neighbor, does not necessarily mean someone related to you by blood, or who lives next door to you. In Matthews 22:39, tells us "to love Thy Neighbor as They self". Instead, we are called higher, to love our brother and sister, to love our neighbor, as Christ loves us. And who is our neighbor? Any human being, because they too are created in the image of God.

If the family is the stone, then the concentric ripples would be local communities,
state, nation, and the world. Thus, it is not enough to merely go home and love
our families. The love we receive there must be carried forth – to the
communities which we are a part of – and in time – to the whole world.

Finally, there things we can do to stop the negative rippling effects:

1. Go home and love your family members. Honor your parents and
grandparents, listen to the stories of your siblings, pray together, forgive
quickly, and be intentional about setting your phone aside and giving them
your undivided attention. Peace begins at home.

2. Make a list of all the communities you are a part of: your Church, school,
clubs, sports, extracurricular, volunteer groups, friends, etc. What role do
you play in each of them? Are you an active member? Or are you a
bystander?

3. What are you passionate about? The environment? Healthy and affordable
food? Providing housing options for the homeless? Promoting racial
justice? Fighting for the unborn? Helping expectant/young mothers? Caring
for the sick? Visiting with the elderly? Helping those who do not easily have
access to education? Volunteer where your heart is. What organization
could join that would allow you to minister to the needs of the vulnerable
members of your community at large?

Finally, for as through one man's disobedience many were made sinners, even so
through the obedience of the one, many will be made righteous. –
Romans 5:19

The above verse references the decisions, and actions of two different men who
lived at different times and how these decisions influenced the lives of many.
When the bible says many, I think it downplays the number of lives that were and
are being affected by their choices. The first man who is referenced to disobey
God was Adam who was placed in the Garden of Eden with his help mate Eden
with the sole responsibilities of communing with God while tending to the
garden.

But unfortunately, he was unable to hold up with his communion and complete
obedience to the Lord. He ate of the tree that he wasn't supposed to touch and
hence he was banished from the garden of abundance. Even worse off, his
children and children's unborn children had to suffer the repercussion of his
singular decision. While on the other hand, Jesus faced with the temptation to
give up on the task given to Him by God drew strength in the place of prayer and
followed through.


Jesus strapped the sins of billions on His shoulders, carried it all
to the cross, and put an end to it all. Because of this daunting, yet single action of
the Lord Jesus Christ, billions of lives were, are, and will be reconciled to our
father in heaven- Romans 5:11-19.

The difference we make in life by following the examples of Christ would send
Ripples to the Ministers family, community, and eventually the world!

Written By
Carey Barnes

Elder at Stonecrest Church of Christ
850 Mount Carmel Road
McDonough, GA 30253

# BISHOP ANTHONY BROOKS

Bishop Anthony Brooks is passionate about serving in the Body of Christ. Originally from Brooklyn, NY, he now resides in Lithia Springs, GA, with his wife, Kellee Brooks. They have been married for over 12 years and have two children: a daughter, Shanice Goode of Greensboro, NC, and a son, Kaleb Brooks, residing in Pensacola Florida. Bishop Brooks has been a devoted member  of the Body of Christ since 1979, beginning

his journey at the Nostrand Ave. congregation in Brooklyn. He has served in various capacities, including worship order, evangelism ministry, and teaching Sunday school and Wednesday night classes for youth and young adults. He also developed and led the Singles Ministry at Hillcrest CoC for over a decade and assisted other singles ministries in the Metro Atlanta area.

# LOVE LANGUAGE: UNDERSTANDING EACH OTHER THROUGH DIFFICULT TIMES TO STRENGTHEN MARRIAGE, BY BISHOP ANTHONY BROOKS

Marriage, a divine covenant established by God, calls for deep understanding, commitment, and love between partners. One powerful framework to help navigate the complexities of marriage is the concept of "Love Languages," popularized by Dr. Gary Chapman. Integrating this framework with biblical teachings, particularly from Ephesians 5:22-33, provides a profound guide for couples seeking to build a stronger, more resilient relationship.

This paper explores how understanding love languages, embracing the scriptural idea of covenant, and practicing unconditional love and respect can fortify marriages, especially during difficult times.

Dr. Gary Chapman identifies five primary love languages: Words of Affirmation, Acts of Service, Receiving Gifts, Quality Time, and Physical Touch. Each individual has a primary love language that, when spoken by their partner, makes them feel most loved and valued. Understanding and speaking each other's love language is crucial in fostering mutual affection and support in marriage.

1. **Words of Affirmation:** Verbal expressions of love, appreciation, and encouragement.

2. **Acts of Service:** Actions that alleviate burdens and show care through helpful deeds.

3. **Receiving Gifts:** Thoughtful presents that demonstrate love and thoughtfulness.

4. **Quality Time:** Undivided attention and meaningful time spent together.

5. **Physical Touch:** Affectionate physical contact, such as holding hands, hugging, or kissing.

By identifying and consistently speaking each other's love language, couples can enhance their emotional connection and resilience during challenging times. This practice builds a solid foundation of understanding and empathy, essential for navigating conflicts and stressors.

Biblical Teachings from Ephesians 5:22-33

The Apostle Paul's teachings in Ephesians 5:22-33 offer a timeless blueprint for marital harmony. Paul calls for wives to submit to their husbands as unto the Lord and for husbands to love their wives as Christ loved the church, giving Himself up for her. This passage highlights the profound spiritual and relational dynamics of marriage.

To truly offer unconditional respect, a wife must first understand what her husband perceives as disrespectful. Disrespect can manifest in various ways, such as dismissing his opinions, undermining his decisions, or criticizing him in public, or it could be as simple as giving an undesirable look. Recognizing these behaviors allows a wife to avoid inadvertently causing hurt or resentment. Importantly, unconditional respect is required even when the wife feels unloved or believes the husband does not deserve it. This is because respect is about honoring God's command and fostering a healthy marital environment, not merely responding to feelings or circumstances.

Likewise, Ephesians 5:25-33 calls husbands to love their wives as Christ loved the church. This love is sacrificial, selfless, and unwavering. Christ's love for the church is the ultimate model of unconditional love, characterized by patience, kindness, and a willingness to put the needs of the wife above personal desires. Husbands are called to cherish their wives, nurturing and caring for them, thus creating an environment of safety and trust.

Unconditional love, as exemplified by Christ, is not contingent on the wife's behavior or worthiness. It is a deliberate choice to love her regardless of circumstances, mirroring Christ's unwavering love for the church even when it falls short. For a husband, this means prioritizing his wife's needs, showing patience during her difficult times, and being kind and supportive even when he feels she does not deserve it. A practical example of loving like Christ involves self-sacrifice. Suppose a husband comes home exhausted from work, but his wife needs help with the children or household chores. Instead of retreating to rest, he chooses to assist her, recognizing that her well-being and the family's harmony are paramount. This act of service demonstrates his commitment to her needs above his own comfort, reflecting Christ's sacrificial love.

Another example is emotional support. If a wife is going through a stressful period and becomes irritable, a husband practicing unconditional love will respond with patience and empathy rather than frustration. He will listen to her concerns, offer comfort, and pray for her, showing her that his love is steadfast and not dependent on her mood or behavior. Husbands must also try to refrain from being in fix it mode when hearing about their wives day to day issues, sometimes she really just wants us to listen to her.

The marriage covenant is a sacred agreement that mirrors God's covenant with His people. It is not merely a contract but a binding commitment that encompasses love, faithfulness, and mutual respect. In a covenantal marriage, couples view their relationship as a divine partnership, dedicated to honoring God through their unity. They must be reminded in conflict that they are working together resolve the conflict together, even when one of them seems to be the conflict. Not always a easy skill to develop in a marriage that has intense conflict to be resolved.

A covenant marriage thrives on the principle of unconditional commitment. Regardless of circumstances, both partners remain devoted to each other, reflecting God's steadfast love. This commitment transcends feelings and situations, focusing on the promise to love, honor, and cherish each other. In a covenant marriage, both partners are willing to make sacrifices for the well-being of the other. This mutual service reflects Christ's sacrificial love and fosters a sense of unity and purpose. By prioritizing each other's needs, couples can navigate difficult times with grace and resilience.

Integrating the concepts of love languages, biblical teachings, and covenant commitment into daily life can significantly enhance marital strength and understanding.

1. Communication: Open and honest communication is vital. Couples should regularly discuss their feelings, needs, and concerns, ensuring that both partners feel heard and valued. Effective communication also involves active listening, empathy, and a willingness to resolve conflicts constructively. They must practice the art of communicating to understand instead of trying to convince to be understood.

2. Learning and Speaking Love Languages: Make a concerted effort to learn and speak each other's love language. This practice involves observing and understanding what makes your partner feel most loved and consistently acting on that knowledge. It may require of you to inquire more specifically from them how do you want to receive this love from me. We can have it in our minds what it looks like but to them it can be totally different, reason this inquiry is so important to not assume you know what their love language means to them.

3. Praying Together: Prayer builds spiritual intimacy, inviting God's guidance and blessings into the marriage. Couples should prioritize praying together, seeking God's wisdom and strength for their relationship. This dedicated prayer time should be intentional and collaborative, focusing on specific concerns. Listening to God's word is also essential, allowing Him to speak to the marriage's needs. This spiritual discipline of prayer and scripture consultation will not only provide wisdom needed for resolving conflicts but will also ensure you walk closely with God. Additionally, it will help you understand each other's weaknesses and align your marriage with God's desires.

4. Regular Check-Ins: Schedule regular times to check in with each other about the state of your marriage. These check-ins, whether weekly, or monthly, should provide a safe space for discussing successes, challenges, and goals. Approach these conversations with an open heart, refraining from judging each other's desires and willingness to invest in the relationship. This non-judgmental environment will foster trust and mutual understanding, helping you to grow together and address issues constructively.

You can do these talks around "date-nights" to lighten the load or feeling of obligation for the conversation to feel so serious. Insert the personality of your relationship during these times, like using phrases that make you both laugh can help take the sting out when someone is on the hot-seat.

5. Supportive Community: Engage with a supportive couple from your church, that can offer encouragement, accountability, and resources. Being part of a church or small group can provide valuable support and perspective. God wired us to depend on community and when your community has the same value system that you and your spouse live by, it will increase your level of success in receiving the aligned wisdom from God's word that is needed. They should also be able to share with you some similar scenarios that you may be going through and offer proper guidance there.

6. Counseling and Mentorship: Seeking professional counseling or mentorship from experienced couples can provide guidance and tools for navigating difficult times. Christian counseling services, such as those offered by Brooks Marriage Counseling Services, can be particularly beneficial in addressing specific issues from a faith-based perspective. When choosing professionals to assist in this area it is very important to seek those with a biblical understanding.
In line with Ephesians 5:22-33, practicing unconditional love and respect is fundamental in strengthening marriage. Unconditional love, as exemplified by husbands, involves selfless devotion and care, mirroring Christ's love for the church. Unconditional respect, as exemplified by wives, involves honoring and valuing the husband's role and efforts.

Unconditional love and respect build a foundation of trust and security in marriage. When both partners feel valued and cherished, they are more likely to open up, share vulnerabilities, and support each other through difficult times. By practicing unconditional love and respect, couples create an environment where both partners can grow and develop. This environment fosters mutual encouragement, understanding, and the pursuit of individual and collective goals. Unconditional love and respect deepen the emotional and spiritual connection between partners. This connection is essential for navigating the challenges of marriage and maintaining a strong, vibrant relationship.

In conclusion, strengthening a marriage requires a multifaceted approach that includes understanding each other's love languages, embracing the scriptural idea of covenant, and practicing unconditional love and respect. By integrating these principles, couples can build a resilient and fulfilling relationship that withstands the trials of life. Ephesians 5:22-33 provides a divine blueprint for marital harmony, emphasizing the importance of selfless love and respect. Through commitment, communication, and a deep spiritual connection, couples can navigate difficult times and emerge stronger, more united, and deeply in love.

# Daniel Carter

From the state
of Mississippi
MINISTERIAL
PROFILE
Evangelist
Daniel Carter
Sr.
7269 Barley
Drive
Ocean Springs,
MS 39564

Married to Sis. Debra Ann Carter

Birthday: July 26, 1958

Mobile: (951) 616-8211

Fax: (800) 685-5010

Email: dcarter0490@yahoo.com

## RELIGIOUS EDUCATION:

**1**    Tutelage under my grandfather, the Late B.T. Martin of the E.21st Avenue Church of Christ in Gary, Indiana

**2**    Ordained to the ministry in 1992 by the Late Evangelist Robert Woods of the Monroe Street Church of Christ

**3**    Installed as Pulpit Minister of the Colonial Village Church of Christ in Chicago, Illinois by the Late Evangelist Robert M. Woods in 1995-2005

**4**    Installed as Co-Minister along with Bro. Roy Williams Jr. at the Church of Christ Eastside in Los Angeles, CA in 2021-2022

**5**    Study Biblical Literature and Biblical History via Southwestern Christian College Online Bible Courses

**6**    Completed the Fishers of Men 13 Week Outreach Program under the oversight of the Elders of the Naperville Church of Christ in Naperville, Illinois


## MINISTERIAL WORKS, EXPERIENCES & AWARDS:

- Supported my grandfather Bro. B.T. Martin for 4 years on a Local Cable Television Program in East Chicago, Illinois called "The Hour of Truth". Continued that work for the next 6 years as the Program Speaker. (Program Director & Videographer was Bro. Connie Williams @ (317) 372-6053)
- Attended the National Annual Lectureship, the Midwest Lectureship, and the Founders Day Lectureship @ Southwestern Christian College in Terrell, Texas.
- Supported the National Crusade for Christ for several years and assisted with Personal Evangelism

 Attended the Midwest Teachers Workshop for 4 years, which originated out of Chicago, Illinois, where I conducted the "New Converts Workshop" for 2 years consecutively.

Currently the Spiritual Director and Overseer of the "National Women of Faith Prayer Line" based out of Moreno Valley, California. (Contact Person can be reached @ 951-505-9274)

Spiritual Director & Counselor for the "Men of Purpose Men's Group" based out of D'Iberville, MS

Author of the "One Shot Personal Evangelism Workshop" of which I have conducted via Power Point for several congregations throughout the brotherhood.

Instructor of the "Wednesday Night Bible Class Series" entitled the "Prison Epistles"

Listed in and Awarded the Outstanding Young Men of America Campaign in 1987

"In all your ways submit to him, and he will make your paths straight."
Proverbs 3:6 (NIV)

**BY EVANGELIST DANIEL CARTER SR.**

# OVERCOMING FEAR AND ANXIETY

We are all prone to fear, anxiety and worry, and when we tell ourselves and then try and convince ourselves that we shouldn't worry about a problem or not be afraid of a fearful situation that we are facing, simply will not make it go away. And so, just telling ourselves and talking to ourselves verbally and audibly about a fear or unwanted problem alone, may even have the tendency to make things worse, and may even prevent us, and can keep us from doing something about it.

But as a Minister of the Lord, and a Gospel Preacher of the word of God, I have concluded that the Bible gives us a specific, and a direct cure for fear and anxiety – and that is to totally and exclusively place our trust in God. We need to learn how to place all of our cares and all of our worries in God's hand. For Peter declares unto us in I Peter Chapter 5 and at verses 6-7 to "Humble yourselves, therefore under God's mighty hand, that he may lift you up in due time. Casting all your anxiety on him because he cares for you"!

Think of it this way, imagine for just a moment, that a particular worry or a certain fear is a heavy burden that you are carrying around on your back (like a backpack filled with heavy rocks). Now, wishing it to go away, or simply telling those rocks to be removed won't solve the problem, nor will it cause the burden to grow lighter.  But suppose you meet someone, who's obviously bigger than you and stronger than you, and either by you asking that person, or that individual volunteers to take the burden off your back, by removing some of the rocks to lighten your load and then carry some of them for you. What would you do? It would be foolish for you to refuse the help and continue to carry that burden alone, but instead, you'd gladly accept the help and would allow that person to share your burden.

WELL, GOD WANTS TO SHARE OUR BURDENS WITH US AS WELL. GOD WANTS TO REMOVE OUR FEARS, CANCEL OUT OUR WORRIES AND GOD WANT'S TO ALLEVIATE ALL OF OUR PAINS, BUT AS THE OLD CLICHÉ GOES, WE MUST LEARN HOW "TAKE OUR BURDENS TO THE LORD AND LEAVE THEM THERE". FOR IT WAS JESUS HIMSELF, WHO DECLARED OVER IN MATTHEW CHAPTER 11 AND AT VERSE 28 THRU 30 HE SAYS; "COME UNTO ME, ALL YE WHO ARE WEARY AND BURDENED, AND I WILL GIVE YOU REST. TAKE MY YOKE UPON AND LEARN FROM ME, FOR I AM GENTLE AND HUMBLE IN HEART, AND YOU SHALL FIND REST FOR YOUR SOULS"!

AND SO, WHEN WE TALK ABOUT "FEAR". WE MUST UNDERSTAND THAT FEAR IS AN UNPLEASANT EMOTION CAUSED BY THE FICTIOUS BELIEF THAT SOMEONE OR SOMETHING HAS DANGEROUSLY BECOME A THREAT TO US, WHICH IN TERMS COULD CAUSE US MENTAL AND PSYCHOLOGICAL PAIN AND SUFFERING. FEAR IS BEING AFRAID OF, OR BEING FRIGHTENED BY SOMETHING THAT EITHER "MAY" OR "MAY NOT" HAPPEN AT ALL. MY WIFE COINED THE PHRASE IN THE FORM OF AN ACRONYM WHICH STATES THAT THE WORD FEAR OR F.E.A.R. STANDS FOR F-FALSE, E-EVIDENCE, A-APPEARING, R-REAL. SOMEONE ELSE HAS ONCE SAID THAT; "THE ONLY THING THAT WE HAVE TO BE AFRAID OF IS FEAR ITSELF"! AND THEN, ONE MUST TAKE NOTE, THAT THE PHRASE "BE NOT AFRAID" APPEARS IN THE BIBLE 365 INDIVIDUAL TIMES, WHICH SAYS THAT GOD GUARANTEES US, AND GOD ASSURES US, AND GOD SPIRITUALLY EQUIPS US WITH A "BE NOT AFRAID" FOR EVERY SINGLE DAY OF THE YEAR.

NOW TO OVERCOME FEAR, AS BELIEVERS IN GOD, WE HAVE TO REALIZE AND BELIEVE IN OUR HEARTS, THAT "WHOEVER IT IS", OR "WHATEVER IT IS" THAT WE MAY BE AFRAID OF, IS UNDER THE POWER AND THE COMPLETE CONTROL OF GOD, FOR THE GOD OF HEAVEN THAT WE SERVE, IS OMNIPOTENT, MEANING THAT GOD IS ALL POWERFUL, AND ALMIGHTY, AND THAT GOD WILL NOT ALLOW ANYTHING TO HAPPEN TO US WITHOUT IT BEING GOD ORDAINED OR GOD PERMITTED. WE FIND AN EXAMPLE OF THIS OVER IN THE 17TH CHAPTER OF THE BOOK OF MATTHEW, WHERE JESUS CAME TO HIS DISCIPLES OUT ON THE SEA, "WALKING ON THE WATER"!  AND IF YOU REMEMBER THE STORY, WHEN PETER AND THE TWELVE FINALLY REALIZED THAT IT INDEED "WAS JESUS" PETER ASKED THE LORD'S PERMISSION TO COME UNTO HIM, AND JESUS SAID "COME"! AND NOW HERE WAS PETER "WALKING ON THE WATER" JUST LIKE JESUS WAS WALKING ON THE WATER, AND AS LONG AS PETER HAD HIS EYES FOCUSED ON JESUS, HE CONTINUED TO WALK UPON THE WATER, BUT THEN THE WINDS STARTED TO BLOW AND THE WAVES STARTED TO CRASH, AND PETER SEEING AND HEARING THESE THINGS, HE TOOK HIS EYES OFF OF CHRIST, AND STARTED LOOKING DIRECTLY AT WHAT HE HAD BECOME AFRAID OF, AND THAT'S WHEN HE BEGAN TO SINK. NOW THE POINT OF ME EXPRESSING ALL OF THIS, IS TO SAY, THAT, WHAT PETER WAS AFRAID OF, JESUS WAS ALREADY WALKING ON IT, IN OTHER WORDS, WHAT MADE PETER AFRAID AND FEARFUL, WAS ALREADY UNDER JESUS'S FEET.

Therefore, when it comes to our fears, and when it comes to things that we are so worried about, it is at these times, and during these moments, that we need to keep our eyes focused on Jesus! According to Hebrews 2:2 we need to always be "Looking unto Jesus, who is the author and the finisher of our faith"!

The Palmist declares in Psalms 121:1, he says; "I will lift up mine eyes unto the hills, from whence cometh my help, for my help cometh from the Lord, which made the heavens and the earth"!

In conclusion, the bible is filled with words of encouragement as well as words of exhortation, to guide our hearts and our minds. Words to strengthen us, words to build us up, and to give us guidance, words to increase our faith, hope and trust in God, enabling us to conquer all doubts, worries and fears. For that great Theologian thee Apostle Paul declares to those young Christian Believers at the church in Philippi, according to Philippians Chapter 4 and at verses 6 and 7, to "Be not anxious for nothing, but in everything by prayer and supplication, with thanksgiving, let your request be made know to God"!

And then who could ever forget that classic example of how Jesus teaches his twelve Disciples over in Matthew Chapter 6 and around verse number 34, when he unto them; "Take therefore no thought for tomorrow, for tomorrow shall take thought for the things of itself. Sufficient unto the day, is the evil thereof"! Simply saying to not be afraid, and not to worry about things that are in the hands of the Lord, the one who has power over things in the earth, under the earth, and above the earth, and who is the God of yesterday, today and tomorrow.

Pastor Christian Fleet
From The State Of Georgia

## TECHNOLOGY IN THE
# *Church*

In the early 2000's I had a vision from the Lord concerning the church in the future. What I had seen was very futuristic and far away at the time. I saw people using their phones to look up scriptures and pay their tithes and offering and this was before smart phones had been invented. I also seen people looking at preachers on screens instead of being in the actual service. I said to myself this was almost impossible because at the time everybody came to church. Over the last twenty years as it seems we see that social media has taken a front seat for a lot of ministries literally putting some of the churches out of commission especially after the pandemic.

If you did not have a social media ministry like Facebook, Youtube, Instagram, or twitter you was almost obsolete. People now a days people find it more convenient to stay at home and do church. People have busy schedules and are to busy to come to a actual building. Though this was convenient during covid; we should be urged to get back to the house of God. The scriptures declare in Hebrews 10:25; To not forsake the assembling of ourselves together as the manner of some is, but exhorting one another; and so much the more, as you see the day approaching. It was the enemy's plan to break us up but we are stronger together. I was glad when they said unto me let us go in the HOUSE OF THE LORD. PSALM 122:1. Oh magnify the LORD with me let us exalt his name together.Psalm 34:1-3 We can do it better together in Jesus name. Be Blessed.

# Minister Franklin Florence The II

From The State Of Florida

## HOW TO TURN YOUR BATTLES INTO BLESSINGS!

2 Chronicles 20:1-3,26

Beloved
I remember hearing a true story that transpired in the metroplex of Paris, France. The Louve is an Internationally renown Musuem, that houses precious art, and artifacts. People all over the world come to see the valuables that are contained within the four walls of the Louve.

There came a time, that an international chess champion came to visit the Louve. For the express purpose of viewing the painting called Checkmate. The painting depicted 2 people playing chess, one resembled the Caricature of the Devil his opponent was disheveled and full of despair.

Based upon the position of the chess pieces on the chess board checkmate was declared. The international chess champion looked at the painting with keen interest, with one arm folded and the other arm and hand resting gently on his chin. The international chess champion both gazed and gawked at the painting and after doing so, for some time he then demanded to see the curator of the museum and shouted this painting must immediately change its name, or be immediately taken down this instance for I am an International chess champion.

The curator after hearing the commotion caused by the International chess champion, he repeated his request for the name change or the immediate removal of the painting for he was in fact an international chess champion. The Curator curiously asked why? He emphatically stated in disgust because the painting entitled checkmate was incorrect. Why the Curator impatiently asked again?

He stated loudly because the King still has one more move! Jesus the Christ and our soon coming King always has one more move!! Soit was and so it is in the life of one named Jehoshaphat. Beloved, the name Jehoshaphat is full of substance and significance. The name Jehoshaphat is a compound word, a compound word is merely when two or more words serveto make up one word the prefix Jeho is an abbreviation for Jehovah or God. The suffix saphat is the Hebrew word meaning to decide in one's favor. (Don't Miss This!)

So every time you say the name Jehoshaphat you are literally saying God has decided and He has decided in my favor. Are you presently facing a stressful situation or you may be in a confining circumstance? Trust and believe, that if you are in fact a committed child of God! Rest assured that God will show you favor by deciding in your favor!

How you may ask? Notice if you will in 2 Chronicles in the B section of verse one we see the word Battle. However in verse twenty six we see the word Blessed better yet Blessings. From my limited post of observation I believe this stress situation begs the question how can I turn my battles into blessings?

Well let's take a look at the text, allow me a moment to make a sagacious suggestion. When reading the Bible always read it carefully, cautiously and completely. In verse one we see Problem People, and problem people are merely people with problems.

 In verse two we see Painful Places, the mere mention of Engedi was a Painful for Jehoshaphat. Finally we see also in verse two, a Paradoxical Predicament. Now a paradox will always occur when two opposites are headed in the same direction.

We are able to see this when we take the time to examine the Hebrew word Hazazon-Tamar. Hazazon means graveyard the place of the dead. Tamar means palm trees or life. Here we have two opposites connected together.

How many times are we guilty of putting on our best Crest toothpaste smile on the outside, when we know we are dying on the inside! How do we react or respond when we battle Problem People, Painful Places, and Paradoxical Predicaments?

In a contextual nutshell we have tone committed to do three tremendous things. We must be willing first and foremost:

1. Look to God!
When trouble comes God can never be viewed as the last resort. If you ever desire to experience God's favor. Don't look to Opra, don't look to Dr Phil look to God! That's what Jehoshaphat did in verses two and three he sought the Lord.

2. Let it Go!
Secondly you have to be willing Praise God; to let it go. In full transparency we are also guilty when we feel we've been mistreated, we have the tendency to hold on to stuff that as Big Mama would say happened 50/11 years ago and act as if it happened yesterday when in fact it transpired years ago! Why should we let it go? The answer comes echoing to us in verse fifteen….For the battle is not your's it's the Lord's

3. Lift Him Up!
Last but not least be willing to lift Him up through worship and praise. Not after the battle has been won, but rather praise Him before the battle has even been fought! That's what I call thanking God on credit, whenever we have enough confidence in Him to thank Him, for the victory before the battle is ample called faith praise, because we fully recognize that there is victory in Jesus!

Beloved the only biblical proven way to turn Battles into Blessings is to Look to God, Let it Go, And to Lift Him Up!

Respectfully Submitted
Franklin Florence ll

# REV. RICKI GARDNER

FROM THE STATE OF FLORIDA

## Pastor & First Lady
## Ricki & Terri Robinson-Gardner

Reverend Ricki Gardner is serving as the current and second Pastor of Christ Missionary Baptist Church, Delray Beach FL, where the late Rev.

Mitchell organized and served for 25 years. Pastor Gardner has led by precept and example. A lover of Christian Education, Pastor Gardner has led us through one mind, one thought with our Membership Enrichment class. Pastor Gardner also honored the founder/former Pastor and wife, Rev Matthew & Martha Mitchell, with our first Christian Leadership School, "The Rev. Matthew & Martha Mitchell CLS Institute" designed to inform, engage, equip and empower the church body for service.

Pastor Gardner, whose vision focuses on the future for the children, is an advocate and supporter of the Youth Department. Pastor has also laid the
foundation for Christ MBC FIRST Women's Ministry and Couples Ministry, with more to come. He is a visionary, Bible
Expositor, with sound doctrine in his preaching and teaching and a lover of souls, and the whole person, and he strives
to help everyone.
Born in Belleville, Ill, a native of Paris TN and the son of the late Rev V. Joseph and Lula M. Gardner, former Moderator of the Obion River District Association

serving two pastorates: Pastor of Mt Zion MBC in Paris, TN for 25 years and Mt Nebo MBC of Clarksville, TN for eight years. His Grandfather, Virgil Gardner served two pastorates in Illinois, making him a third-generation pastor/preacher.

He is blessed with a beautiful God fearing and loving wife, Terri Michelle, two adult daughters, Uneka and Iona and three grandchildren, TeShaun, Arianna, Skye, and a godson, Dylan Wright. Prior to relocating to Boynton Beach Rev. Gardner was the organizer/pastor of The Church of Grand Prairie in Dallas, Texas where he served for 13 years, as an Associate Minister of the Mount Moriah Missionary Baptist Church in Dallas 11years, served as Senior Pastor of Ebenezer Missionary Baptist Church in Boca Raton for two years, and Shady Grove Missionary Baptist Church in Coconut Grove where he served one year.

 Gardner formerly served humbly on the ministerial staff at St. John Missionary Baptist Church in Boynton Beach, Florida for five years as the Director of Christian Education. Rev. Gardner was part of the church vision under the leadership of the late Rev Lance Chaney that has brought bountiful blessings, and phenomenal growth with over 2500 members. His responsibilities included Sunday school, New Members Orientation, Men's Ministry, Women's Ministry, Evangelism, Nursery, Teen Bible Study, Y.I.P. (Youth In Praise), Missions and the educational needs of all other auxiliaries of St. John Pastor Gardner has faithfully served in the Florida East Coast Baptist Association as where he served as Secretary of Missions under past Moderator Dr. C.P. Preston Jr., assistant to Rev. Calvin Davis former Northern Union President. Under past Congress President Rev Jeffrey Mack, Rev. Gardner served as past Director General for the Florida East Coast Congress and now as Dean of Record under the Congress President Benjamin Parrot, Dean Dr. Joyce Dunlap, and past servant leader of Pastors and Ordained minister's instructor under the past Northern Union President, Rev. Benjamin Carroll.

Rev. Gardner has received many honors and awards marking his accomplishments and contributions to the State of Texas, Florida and beyond. He has earned two Bachelors (Interdisciplinary Studies and Theology), and four Masters Degrees (Non-Profit Management, Higher Education Administration, Christian Education and Divinity. Those labors afforded him numerous opportunities to serve as an advocate and faculty at the South Florida Bible College and Theological Seminary in Deerfield Beach, FL. Pastor Gardner is also a Nationally Certified Dean with the Sunday School Publishing Board, and serves as Faculty in the FL East Coast, Florida General Baptist, and National Baptist Congresses of Christian Education. Walking the Talk; Maintaining Authenticity with Your Spouse and ministry Integrity in Leadership Roles by Pastor Ricki Gardner.

I have served with fervor and joy in ministry for over 30 years. In reflection, I am reminded of the passage, "Remain in the place of your calling" I Cor. 7:20. When I first accepted my "calling" (from which I ran for 18 years), I wanted to sing in the choir AND preach, but the Lord reminded me that He called me to preach...not sing!!!

Walking the talk with authenticity and integrity, is to first make sure that you are operating in your calling in which the Holy Spirit has placed you. Knowing this will ensure that you are authorized and empowered to carry out the work of the Lord. Once established, two passages come to mind. First, Phil. 2:5-11 command us to let this mind be IN you which was also in Christ Jesus, with the following verses showing us how to present ourselves. Second, Col. 3:16 commands that we allow the word of Christ dwell (live) in us richly (saturation). Please take note of the two parallels given, mind and word. Having the mind of Christ simply means that we need to think like Jesus and word informs us that those thoughts are based on word- the Word of God.

Just because we are "saved", does not mean we are exempt from the troubles of this world. In fact. A common mistake which overtakes many serving in ministry, is they feel they are "exempt" from faults, failures, and frailties. Also to note, we have an enemy, the world, the flesh, and the devil. Since we are fallen flesh to begin with, we are always subjected to the three L's; lust of the eyes, lust of the flesh, and the pride of life (yes, pride is a form of lust as well). To deny their existence is to set yourself up for failure. There is no shortage of evidence of this lying all around us...right in the church itself. Yes, there are biblical examples such as Lot, David, and Saul, and modern-day people in the news and right around the corner from us. They sit in pulpit, lead worship, teach Church school classes and so on...no shortage! One thing they all have in common, they suffer from the elixir of the three L's of fallen humanity.

By allowing (and you must submit yourselves daily) the word of Christ to dwell in us richly and the mind of Christ (the word of Christ and the mind never contradicts each other)requires a saturation of our souls, enabling us with the spiritual tools necessary to maintain a life of transparency, and our commitment to Christ. Our relationship with each other should be reflected through the 'outliving' if the indwelling Holy Spirit. I have not always been who I am now, but one thing I did learn before I came into the ministry, was the destruction and collateral damaged cause to individuals and families from the lack of authenticity, transparency, and commitment, which leads to a breach of integrity in ministry.

Does not the Bible say that a little leaven affects t w whole lump (Gal 5:9)? I Cor. 6:19-20 reminds us that our bodies are the temple (house) of the Holy Spirit, that we received from God, and we no longer own ourselves (we never did to begin with, ALL humanity belongs to God by right of creation), and we were purchased by God through the blood of His Son, so we ought to honor God with our bodies.

Remember this, ALL unrighteousness is sin (I John 5:17a) and sin will carry you farther than you want to go, keep you longer than you want to stay, and cost you more than you want to pay—Gardner. Ministry can be taxing, consuming, and has its' own unique challenges. Real ministry and real leadership begin at home. As my mother used to say, "Charity (love) begins at home, then spreads abroad." In other words, you are not operating in authenticity and integrity if things are not right at home. Authenticity requires transparency and vulnerability, because if you are not real with each other about the realities of relationships (and our God is relational), how can we maintain integrity in ministry?

The platform, or filter for integrity in ministry begins with being authentic with your spouse. The world, the flesh, and the Devil seek to destroy the authenticity of the relationship which will in turn destroy the integrity in ministry. Remember, Charity (agape-love) begins at home, and then spreads abroad.

# MINISTER
## JOE DARRELL GIBBS, SR.

From the state of Texas

TEMPTATION IS REAL

Minister Joe Darrell Gibbs, Sr.
Minister at the Avenue .K.
Church of Christ
3209 Avenue .K.
Fort Wirth Texas 76105

It has been stated that "You will discover through the scripture that these are always the big temptations. John calls them "The lust of the eye, the lust of the flesh, and the boastful pride of life" (1 John 2:16). When Jesus was outlining what men must surrender to follow Him, these 3 issues are what He addresses (Luke 14:25-35)"

Research suggests that "Real temptation is when your values are being tested and what you believe is right. To be tempted is to do the wrong thing. It is against your inner grounded beliefs"

The subject of temptation , in and of itself, is a jarring point of mediation that immediately causes one to analyze where he or she stands within nuances of the word itself. I purport this because temptation causes a serious debate within our minds. This debate concerns how we view our personal standing within the confines of temptation. In other words, are we dealing with being tempted or have we become a victim of the result of temptation. This is a critical question to the serious server of God. In my view,

It is easy to digest the definition of temptation but it is all together a different challenge to know exactly where we are in relation to whether or not we have succomed to its mighty grip. Yes, temptation has a strong magnetic force that is easy to become a victim of, and each of us is confronted with temptation each day of our lives. The question is: To what degree has temptation persuaded us to consciously deny one's self-centered gratification in order to please God or ourselves.

"The Scriptures tell us that we all face temptations. First Corinthians 10:13 says, "No temptation has overtaken you but such as is common to man." Perhaps this provides a little encouragement as we often feel that the world is bearing in on us alone, and that others are immune to temptations. We are told that Christ was also tempted: "For we do not have a high priest who cannot sympathize with our weaknesses, but One who has been tempted in all things as we are, yet without sin" (Hebrews 4:15)."

That great apostle to the Gentiles, Paul, said, Resist the devil and he will fleet from you. while this is true, is does not mean the devil will leave you forever because he always come back with another level of temptation.  In closing, I reassert that Temptation is Real but if we arm ourselves with spiritual discernment and with the whole armour of God. Listen to what the apostle Paul provides us as a reason to know that even-tough Temptation is Real, God assures us that His protection of His redeemed children is real also!

Eph 6:10-8. Listen…

 Finally, be strong in the Lord and in his mighty power. 11 Put on the full armor of God,so that you can take your stand against the devil's schemes. 12 For our struggle is not against flesh and blood, but against the rulers, against the authorities, against the powers of this dark world and against the spiritual forces of evil in the heavenly realms. 13 Therefore put on the full armor of God, so that when the day of evil comes, you may be able to stand your ground, and after you have done everything, to stand. 14 Stand firm then, with the belt of truth buckled around your waist, with the breastplate of righteousness in place, 15 and with your feet fitted with the readiness that comes from the gospel of peace. 16 In addition to all this, take up the shield of faith, with which you can extinguish all the flaming arrows of the evil one. 17 Take the helmet of salvation and the sword of the Spirit, which is the word of God.

# In the Business of
# Inclusivity

A short intro or kicker of the article will go here. This part acts as a bridge between the headline and the article itself.

By Margarita Perez.
Photography by Francois Mercer

And pray in the Spirit on all occasions with all kinds of prayers and requests. With this in mind, be alert and always keep on praying for all the Lord's people.

# TEMPTATION IS REAL

# Minister Tolliver

From Coliseum Boulevard Church of Christ From the state of North Carolina

"Then he said to his disciples,
'The harvest is plentiful but the workers are few.'"
Matthew 9:37

# PASSING THE TORCH

My humble beginnings originated in my hometown of Nashville Tennessee. I was raised by my paternal aunt and uncle. My uncle was a minister in a methodist Church. After attending a tent meeting and being mentored by the late Brother Alonzo Rose my uncle left denomination and became minister of the Green Street Church of Christ in Nashville in the early 60s. I remembered my uncle's teachings and credit my Christian foundation in part, to the tutelage of that great Sunday School teacher, the late Sister Essie T. Battle.

While attending Tennessee State University, I was drafted for the Vietnam War. I served two years in the Army and by the grace of God, I never saw Vietnam. As a young man I had no intentions of becoming a Minister…. but our plans are not God's plans. (Isaiah 55:8-10). At the time, I didn't realize my uncle had already passed the torch. After leaving the military, I relocated to south Florida and began attending the Hallandale Beach Church of Christ in Hallandale Beach Florida where I participated in song leading and teaching. In1975, I was hired as the interim Evangelist and later became the full-time Evangelist of the congregation until 1981.

During my tenure at Hallandale Beach COC the leadership was instrumental in supporting my ministry allowing me to grow. Over these past forty-nine years, I have held full-time Evangelist positions for congregations in Wisconsin, Alabama, Texas, Tallahassee, Florida and High Point, North Carolina. In 1994, after much prayer, I took a leap of faith and with the torch in hand, burning with fire I planted a new congregation in Greensboro, NC. I am currently the pulpit minister of the Coliseum Boulevard Church of Christ in Greensboro. This congregation begun from two congregations merging in 2000.

As a seasoned minister the time has come to make a maturational change.
Before the end of this year, Coliseum Boulevard Church of Christ will appoint a new pulpit, minister. Deuteronomy 31:1 34:5-9 conveys THEY are to pass the torch, and to do so, they must first have the torch themselves and be burning which is indicative of a personal relationship with GOD.

Throughout my time as an Evangelist, a torch has been passed to me. My
remarkable spiritual father, the late Brother Robert Woods mentored, coached and prayed for me. I learned from him that a Christian cannot grow spiritually without the mentorship of another Christian sharing and
teaching sound doctrine. I have trusted God, persevered and pressed through. I possess knowledge and wisdom beneficial to my successor. I am now passing the torch. (Psalms: 78 1-8) It is only fitting that I pass the torch. Apostle Paul had this idea in mind when he encouraged his young protégé, Timothy. Passing the torch is a metaphor from ancient Greek torch with several meanings, for me the expression reflects an older generation passing to a younger generation, a transfer of leadership.
I believe God's objective for my exit from full time preaching is not to retire but to repurpose my Ministry.

 I will continue the Facebook ministry class on Tuesday evenings "What Sayeth the Scriptures" under the banner, Jesse Tolliver's Outreach Ministries. I will offer spiritual support throughout the brotherhood. I am available to preach and teach God's word to congregations in need of temporary support, respite, gospel meetings, lectureships and/or workshops. As a "traveling Evangelist" I will continue to contend for the faith. Mostly, I am trusting God's plans for my life as "Torchbearer"! (Romans 1:16) Jesse Tolliver III Evangelist, Coliseum Boulevard Church of Christ Brother Tolliver is married to the former Debra Washington. They have a blended family of five adult children and are grandparents to seven amazing grandchildren.

# MINISTER GEORGE WHITE

From The State Of Georgia

SPOTLIGHT SPECTUALR MAGAZINE

As Evangelist for the Churches of Christ, Brother George White III is married to his loving wife, Mary, and has Preached the gospel of Christ for over 30 years. Brother White holds an Associate of Science degree in Business from Southwestern Christian College, in Terrell, Tx.:
A Bachelor of Arts in Religion from Pepperdine University, in Malibu California, A Bachelor of Arts in Human Services from Mercer University:
A Master of Business (MBA) from the University of Phoenix, and A Master of Divinity (M.Div.) in Theology from Emory University, in Atlanta, Georgia. Brother White is also a certified Chaplain, having completed the necessary credit hours of Clinical Pastoral Education (CPE) from Emory Hospital, in Atlanta, GA, where he also served as a Chaplain for several years. Both Brother and Sister White currently serve the College Park Church of Christ, in East Point, Georgia.

Building for Eternity
{Building with Resilient through Faith, Matthew 7: 24}

"Whosoever heareth these sayings of mine, and doeth them, I will liken him unto a wise man, which built his house upon a rock: And the rain descended, and the floods came, and the winds blew, and beat upon that house; and it fell not: for it was founded upon a rock.
And everyone that heareth these sayings of mine, and doeth them not, shall be likened unto a foolish man, which built his house upon the sand: And the rain descended, and the floods came, and the winds blew, and beat upon that house; and it fell: and great was the fall of it" (KJV).
Everyone knows a house must be built… Everyone also knows that it takes a certain amount of wisdom to build a house. Unfortunately, not everyone knows the proper way to lay a good foundation to build a house. Therefore, not everyone can successfully build a house.
Likewise, when building a "successful life," whether one's physical life or spiritual, this same principle is true; you must be sure that you're building on a sure foundation. Therefore, the Bible likens the idea of receiving eternal salvation when we die to a person who has the skill to know how to build.
Noah built an "Ark," and, from a flood, eight souls were saved. Abraham built an "altar" to worship or "call on" God's name. Moses built the "Tabernacle," King David established "the Israeli nation," and Jesus has built "the Church" for salvation of every nation. Therefore, for our daily lives to know victory, and our souls to ultimately be saved, we too must make sure that we build on a sure foundation. If you don't believe you have some "building" to do, just remember what Jesus has said: "Not everyone that says, 'Lord, Lord,' shall enter into the kingdom of heaven, but the one who does the will of my Father, which is heaven, (Matthew 7:21). We must do God's will to build.

Since most of us have already started building our lives the question is now begged,
"can a damaged house be repaired?" In other words, can the "alcoholic" ever stop juicing? Can a "dope-attic" ever quit shooting? Can a "hooker" ever stop selling? Can even an "ex-con" make it to heaven? Can a "thief" cease from stealing? Will the
"pusher" ever stop dealing? Those hooked on sin today want to know is it possible for them to change?

With God all things are possible! Thus, the "sayings of Jesus" provides the necessary wisdom to start us over and rebuild the broken foundations our lives. The
Apostle Paul said that "the foolishness of God is wiser than men" (I Corinthians 1:25).
Therefore, like a good foundation, "the sayings of Jesus" are as solid as a rock.
Jesus said, "Whoever hears the sayings of mine, and does them, I will liken him unto a wise man, which built his house upon a rock: And the rain descended, and the floods came, and the winds blew, and beat upon that house; and it fell not: for it was founded upon a rock.
Wise people allow Jesus to repair and restore the foundations of their lives, because
Jesus is in the "transforming business!" You see God formed us, but sin has deformed us. Prisons attempt to reform us, while schools work to inform us, but only Jesus can transform us from brokenness and rejections, death and bereavements,
and pain and loneliness. Only Jesus can deliver us from relationship failures and various emotional, psychological and substance abuses to an abundant life.
I invite you to seek the counsel of the LORD. He will pardon our past and protect our present when we apply to our lives the power in the counsel of God's word. The
scripture says, "Seek the LORD while He may be found, call upon Him while He is near. Let the wicked forsake His way, and the unrighteous one his thoughts: and let
him return unto the LORD, and the LORD will have mercy upon him; and our God, He will abundantly pardon!"
Always remember the words of the Apostle Paul: "According to the grace of God, which is given unto me, as a wise Master Builder, I have laid the foundation, and another builds thereon. But let every man take heed how he builds thereupon.
For other foundation can no man lay than that is laid, which is Jesus Christ.
Now if any man builds upon this foundation gold, silver, precious stones, wood, hay, stubble, every man's work shall be revealed: for the day shall declare it, because it shall be revealed by fire; and the fire shall try every man's work of what sort it is.
If any man's work abides which he hath built thereupon, he shall receive a reward" (I Corinthians 3:10-14).
Ministering Evangelist, George White III, M.Div.

# MINISTER MICHAEL . PEAVY

## FROM CHICAGO ILLINOIS

EVANGELIST, GOLGOTHA CHURCH OF CHRIST

CERTIFIED CHAPLAIN

"LET US NOT BECOME WEARY IN DOING
GOOD, FOR AT THE PROPER TIME WE
WILL REAP A HARVEST IF WE DO NOT
GIVE UP." GALATIANS 6:9

From the Pulpit to the Neighborhood: Extending the Reach of Faith throughout the Community, Emphasizing the Importance of Outreach Services, Building Relationship

beyond Church Walls.

Living in this post-COVID era, mankind is in chronic dire need of CPR, Cardio-Pulmonary Resuscitation. In order to avoid flatlining, remaining static, or becoming so near to death that our vital signs from the heavenly ECG (electrocardiogram) display a failure to increase or produce fruit for the Lord. It is of utmost importance that we work diligently at building relationships within the community that we reside in to reach beyond the church walls.

Nevertheless, my aim of importance is at finetuning our understanding of effectiveness in order to prune our awareness toward improvement in health, wellness, airflow and direct new growth. Congruently, we will look at the defining nature for the following seven questions: What

is community? Who is my neighbor? What is the purpose of a neighborhood? How do I become

effective within my neighborhood? How do I extend the reach of faith throughout the community? Is it realistic to move from the pulpit to the neighborhood? And, why are outreach services important?

What is community? The Oxford Dictionary defines community as "a group of people living in the same place or having a particular characteristic in common. A feeling of fellowship with others, as a result of sharing common attitudes, interests, and goals." Yet, more defining, a biblical community is where we are to come alongside each other to grow and mature our faith.

A biblical community should be a co-building Christian community where all the people in the grouping work to follow the teachings of Jesus Christ. It is an opportunity to show each other, and a world of onlookers, the true love of God. Furthermore, maturing or developing our growing faith in God opens up a window for the world to look through to see the true agapao of God.

PAUL INFORMS US IN ROMANS 12:4-5 (KJV), "FOR AS WE HAVE MANY MEMBERS IN ONE BODY, AND ALL MEMBERS HAVE NOT THE SAME OFFICE: SO WE, BEING MANY, ARE ONE BODY IN CHRIST, AND EVERY ONE MEMBERS ONE OF ANOTHER." CONSEQUENTLY, IT IS WITHIN THIS POPULACE POOL OF BELIEVER'S THAT SEEDS OF DIVISION ARE SPREAD OUT TRYING TO BE PLANTED BY THE ENEMY. WE MUST STAY ALERT. WE MUST STAY AWAKE. AWAKE ENOUGH TO BE ABLE TO GUARD AGAINST THE APPEARANCE OF SUCH. "NOW I BESEECH YOU, BRETHREN, BY THE NAME OF OUR LORD JESUS CHRIST, THAT YE ALL SPEAK THE SAME THING, AND THAT THERE BE NO DIVISIONS AMONG YOU; BUT THAT YE BE PERFECTLY JOINED TOGETHER IN THE SAME MIND AND IN THE SAME JUDGMENT" (1 CORINTHIANS 1:10).

THIS PUSHES ME TO ASK THE QUESTION, WHO IS MY NEIGHBOR? THE WORLD WE LIVE IN TODAY HAS OVER THE YEARS CONTINUALLY CHANGED FOR THE WORST. IT IS NOT EVOLVING TOWARD BETTERMENT. WITH TECHNOLOGY, SCIENCE AND ARTIFICIAL INTELLIGENCE SKYROCKETING AT A LASER'S PACE IN TIME, OUR CHILDREN ARE NOW GOING TO SCHOOL WITH METAL DETECTORS, LESS NUTRITIOUS MEALS AND CONSUMING A DIET FILLED PEAVY 2 WITH STEROID PROCESSED MEATS, PUMPED UP FRUITS & VEGETABLES, MINIMAL PHYSICAL ACTIVITY WHICH HAS EXACERBATED OBESITY WITH DIABETIC SICKNESS, AND NO REAL OUTLOOK ON FUTURE GOALS.

VIOLENT VIDEO GAMES HAVE NOW BEEN EMPLOYED AS NEW MILLENNIUM BABYSITTERS; AND A SENSE OF BELONGING HAS NOW BECOME QUESTIONABLE AND MORE DIFFICULT TO INTERLOCK WITH. AS A RESULT OF ALL THIS, OUR YOUTH ARE BEING RADICALLY ESCALATED AS JAILED, HOSPITALIZED, WOUNDED AND/OR KILLED AT AN ASTRONOMICAL RATE. THE HOME HAS BEEN SHATTERED LIKE GLASS. THE CONCENTRATION ON EDUCATION IS OF LOW IMPORTANCE. AND, ACCEPTABLE DISRESPECT IS SHOVELED IN AT AN ALL-TIME HIGH. EVEN PARTICIPANTS OF PROTESTS HAVE ORDERED AND ARE NOW WEARING THE PRINTED T-SHIRT OF RAINBOW DIVERSITY. IT IS THROUGH THIS MIRROR OF DYSFUNCTION AND MUDDY DISAPPEARANCE OF LOVE THAT JESUS HELPS US TO SPECIFICALLY RECOVER, DISCOVER AND UNCOVER EXACTLY WHO OUR NEIGHBOR IS AND WHO OUR NEIGHBOR IS NOT TO BE. THE GEOGRAPHICAL SETTING OF LUKE 10:25-37 HAS BECOME AN 18-MILE TREK OR 39 KILOMETERS OF WAR ZONE FROM JERUSALEM TO JERICHO. THIS IS RELATABLE TO MANY OF US LIVING IN CITIES OR AREAS OF TOWN WHERE THE SAFETY OF YOUR TERRITORY IS BEING DEFINED BY EVERY 4 TO 8 BLOCKS OF GANG TERRITORY.

Jesus says in verse 30 that "a certain man went down from Jerusalem to Jericho, and fell among thieves, which stripped him of his raiment, and wounded him, and departed, leaving him half dead." This sounds like the first ten (10) minutes of any modern-day local news broadcast. Half dead does not always equate to being half alive. Question: What are the identifying attributes of reliable help one must look for when faced with real trouble? Jesus informs us in this parable of The Good Samaritan that it is not always who you think it should be. He also teaches us that our true neighbor might just be the one society has degraded; the one society has dumped on in the past; but now, experiencing the emotional merciful heart of God, one who forgets what is unimportant to society and focuses on what is important a hand, a friend in need. A friend indeed helps a friend in need. My neighbor is the one who will emancipate and deliver me when it is so needed. A friend indeed! Verse 33 says, "But a certain Samaritan, as he journeyed, came where he was: and when he saw him, he had compassion on him, and went to him, and bound up his wounds, pouring in oil and wine, and set him on his own beast, and brought him to an inn, and took care of him.

And on the morrow when he departed, he took out two pence, and gave them to the host, and said unto him, Take care of him; and whatsoever thou spendest more, when I come again, I will repay thee." Once we learn and apply the attributes of this principle, we too will gain strength, power and the ableness to make change in the world we live in today.

What is the purpose of a neighborhood? As we begin to demonstrate God's vision of empathic community, the Bible tells us "To love our neighbors as we love ourselves" (Mark 12:31). The more we crave to study the word of God, debar Adonai, the more we devote ourselves to more biblical truth. "All scripture is given by the inspiration of God, and is profitable for doctrine, for reproof, for correction, for instruction in righteousness: that the man of God may be perfect (mature), thoroughly furnished unto all good works" (2 Timothy 3:16-17). As we encourage perseverance of one another in the faith, more abundantly we will gain and maintain a posture of love that reflects God. God is the glory the world must see. We are reflectors of utility for God to this world. How do I become effective within my neighborhood? By loving my neighbor as I love myself. The more I learn to love me; the more I will directly learn to love my neighbor. Paul tells us to esteem others above myself (Philippians 2:3-5). Peter helps us with this in 1 Peter 4:9, "Use hospitality one to another without grudging." How do I extend the reach of faith throughout the community? By demonstrating hospitality to whomever I come in contact with. Let us be active love agents to welcome people into our lives (Romans Peavy 3 15:7), regardless of their appearance (James 2:1-4), regardless of their heritage and background (Acts 10:34-35), and more importantly, regardless of whether or not they are able to help us in return (Luke 6:34-35). Fred Rogers, from the PBS television show Mr. Roger's Neighborhood, would respond when posed with the question of who are the people in your neighborhood.

HE CONSTANTLY REPLIED, "THEY ARE THE PEOPLE THAT YOU MEET WHEN YOU ARE WALKING DOWN THE STREET; THEY ARE THE PEOPLE THAT YOU MEET EACH DAY." EVEN JESUS HIMSELF RESPONDED TO AN ATTORNEY THAT LEARNED THE TRUE MEANING OF SHOWING MERCY. JESUS SAYS, "GO, AND DO THOU LIKEWISE" (LUKE 10:37). WHY ARE OUTREACH SERVICES IMPORTANT? WE THANK GOD FOR THE PLETHORA OF GOVERNMENT AND LOCAL PROGRAMS THAT EXIST TODAY. AT THE BLINK OF AN EYE, TRAGEDY CAN INSTANTANEOUSLY OVERTAKE ANY OF US. IT SEEMS TO BE THAT EVERY TERRITORY STRUGGLES WITH THE PAINS OF SETBACK AND DISASTER. OUTREACH AIDES TO MEND THE HEART OF PEOPLE. OUTREACH IS JUST THAT, A REACH OUTWARDLY, A STRETCHED-OUT ARM FROM HEAVEN TO ASSIST MAN IN SPECIFIC WAYS AND MANNERS. JOHN 3:16 INFORMS US THAT JESUS IS THE OMNIPOTENT ENSAMPLE OF OUTREACH MINISTERIAL SERVANTHOOD.

THE PSALMIST SAYS, "SING UNTO THE LORD, BLESS HIS NAME; SHEW FORTH HIS SALVATION FROM DAY TO DAY. DECLARE HIS GLORY AMONG THE HEATHEN, HIS WONDERS AMONG ALL PEOPLE" (PSALM 96:2-3). OUTREACH SERVICES HELP, UPLIFTS, AND SUPPORTS THOSE WHO ARE IN NEED OR HAVE BEEN DEPRIVED OF CERTAIN SERVICES AND INDIVIDUAL RIGHTS. LASTLY IN REASON, IS IT REALISTIC TO MOVE FROM THE PULPIT TO THE NEIGHBORHOOD?

HOW DO WE FIGHT BACK AGAINST THE PRESENT DECLINE IN CHURCH ATTENDANCE, AN INCREASINGLY NON-RELIGIOUS POPULATION OF PEOPLE, AND AN ENORMOUS NUMBER OF CHURCHES CLOSING THEIR DOORS SINCE THE ACCELERATION OF COVID? HOW DO WE INCORPORATE THE TRUTH OF THE GOSPEL TO A WORLD FULL OF CURRENT REBELLION AND CONSTANT CHANGE? FIRST AND FOREMOST, WE MUST RECOGNIZE THE SENSE OF URGENCY TRIAGED BEFORE US. SECONDLY, WE MUST BECOME THAT LIGHT, THAT VISIBLE VOICE OF HOPE THAT GOD NAVIGATES AND REGULATES CHANGE THROUGH. "YE ARE THE LIGHT OF THE WORLD. A CITY THAT IS SET ON AN HILL CANNOT BE HID" (MATTHEW 5:14). WE MUST NOT GROW WEARY IN WELL-DOING. RATHER, THANK GOD FOR THE OPPORTUNITIES HE HAS PLACED BEFORE YOU (PHILIPPIANS 4:13). THEN, WE MUST IMPLEMENT LOVE IN EVERYTHING WE DO, EVERY STEP OF THE WAY KNOWING THAT THE LORD WILL LEAD US; THE LORD WILL PROTECT US; THE LORD WILL GUIDE US (PSALM 23:1-6).

# National School of Theology

by authority of the board of trustees and upon recommendation of the faculty

hereby confers upon

## Michael Peavy

the Degree of

## Associate of Christian Counseling

Together with all the rights, privileges and honors appertaining to therein in recognition of the satisfactory completion of the courses prescribed by the faculty of the seminary

In testimony whereof the undersigned have subscribed their names and affixed their seal given in Dover, Delaware this thirtieth day of July, two thousand and twenty-four.

Orlando Short

Pamela Elliott-Hubbard

Pamela Copper

Ronald Fisher

Ephesians 3:20: "Now to him who is able to do immeasurably more than all we ask or imagine, according to his power that is at work within us"

**MINISTER ROBERT L TURNER – JACKSON BOULEVARD COC**

**SISTER GLADYS TURNER**

## FROM THE STATE OF CHICAGO

**1-773-826-1872**
**3355 W. JACKSON BLVD**
**CHICAGO, IL, 60624**

Bro. Robert L. Turner has been married to Sis. Gladys Turner for 51 years and they were blessed with four wonderful children, 15 grandchildren. He is a faithful servant to our Lord, Jesus Christ, and has been preaching the gospel for over 32 years, serving as Minister of Jackson Blvd. Church of Christ for the past 16 years. Bro. Turner is an advocate of higher education, always encouraging Jackson Blvd.'s family to increase their knowledge personally but more importantly spiritually. Bro. Turner remains active within the Church of Christ brotherhood, facilitating for many years the Chicago-land Preachers Breakfast and serves as the Chicagoland local coordinator for the National Crusade for Christ for over 10 years, facilitating the United Bible Class for over 15 years and serves as Spiritual Advisor for Levi Kennedy Scholarship Committee. Jackson adopted the theme "Serving Man that leads to Saving Man" and our congregational focus is to be an influence in the community that will help to empower this philosophy. Bro. Turner is continually making his presence known in his community as an elected Trustee since 1997 -2021 and served as Chairman over the Building and Health Department in Calumet Park, IL. Whether serving the Lord's people or the community Bro. Turner does it with joy. His faith is rooted and grounded in the power of God and not the wisdom of men.

SISTER GLADYS TURNER is married to that singing Gospel Preacher Bro. Robert L. Turner, minister/servant of the Jackson Blvd. Church of Christ in Chicago, Illinois. The Lord has blessed Sister Gladys Turner to be an active part of Jackson Blvd. Church of Christ Congregation. She serves as one of the Coordinators of the Ladies Ministry and Ladies Bible Class. Gladys has been a blessing helping her husband on their theme of "Membership Empowerment". She also serves the Bowser Women working for SWCC and as a staff member for the Chicagoland National Crusade for Christ. In addition, she has conducted seminars on marriage and grief. Sister Gladys Turner has also spoken on several Ladies Day Programs. She attended Alabama State University in Montgomery, Alabama. Gladys has also served as a Community Relations Commissioner for years in Calumet Park, Illinois. Her favorite scripture is; Romans 8:28 "And we know that all things work together for the good of them that love the Lord and who are the called according to His purpose".

# LIVING WITH A PURPOSE - TWO NATURES IN US
## ROMANS 7: 13-25

**Jackson Boulevard Church of Christ**

There is inside all of us two natures. One to do good and one to do evil. Two natures, one that is dominant and one that is subservient. Two natures in us, one that rules and one that is ruled. Two natures in us, one that is seen and one not seen. Two natures in us, the flesh and the spirit. Most of our life and time is spent on feeding the fleshly nature and not the spirit. We love to dress up and nourish the fleshly nature of man. We are concerned how it looks to other people. This fleshly nature of man loves and craves to be fed and clothed and taken care of on a daily basis and we do. The spirit nature of man also deserves to also be clothed and fed, for it is the part of man that God desires to dwell in. This is the nature of man that should be become dominant and rule in man. I am reminded of a story of two dogs in a fight. This owner always knew which dog would win the fight. Every time the two dogs would fight, the owner always knew which dog would win. The people were much perplexed and could not figure out why. And so, the owner finally revealed to them how he always knew. He simply said, the one I feed the most is the one that always win. The point or moral of the story is; whatever nature we feed the most, the flesh or the spirit will always win the fight. Most of our time is spent on taking care of and feeding the flesh and not the spirit of man.

ONE REASON IS THAT MEN LOVE DARKNESS MORE THAN LIGHT. JOHN 3: 19-21; "AND THIS IS THE CONDEMNATION, THAT LIGHT IS COME INTO THE WORLD, AND MEN LOVED DARKNESS RATHER THAN LIGHT, BECAUSE THEIR DEEDS WERE EVIL, FOR EVERY
ONE THAT DOETH EVIL HATETH THE LIGHT, NEITHER COMETH TO THE LIGHT, LEST HIS DEEDS SHOULD BE REPROVED. BUT HE THAT DOETH TRUTH COMETH TO THE LIGHT, THAT HIS DEEDS MAY BE MADE MANIFEST, THAT THEY ARE WROUGHT IN GOD". IF MAN DOES NOT CONTROL HIS FLESH, HIS FLESH WILL CONTROL HIM. MAN IN HIS OWN POWER AND STRENGTH WILL ALWAYS LOOSE THE FIGHT BECAUSE SIN WILL ALWAYS DOMINATE HIM. MAN, THEREFORE NEEDS THE SPIRIT OF GOD TO OVERCOME THE SPIRIT OF THE FLESH, BECAUSE THERE IS
CONSTANTLY A WAR GOING ON BETWEEN THE FLESH AND THE SPIRIT OF MAN. PAUL IN ROMANS 6: 14 HAD EARLIER PENNED THAT "SIN SHALL NOT HAVE DOMINION OVER YOU, FOR YE ARE NOT UNDER THE LAW BUT UNDER GRACE". ROMANS 7: 13-23 IS A GREAT EXAMPLE OF THE BATTLE BETWEEN THE FLESH AND THE SPIRIT.

PAUL DESIRED TO DO GOOD, BUT IN HIM WAS ANOTHER DESIRE TO DO EVIL. THE THINGS HE WANTED TO DO, HE FOUND HIMSELF NOT DOING AND THE THINGS HE DID NOT WANT TO DO, WERE THE VERY THINGS HE FOUND HIMSELF  DOING. THE POWER OF SIN AND THE FLESHLY NATURE OF MAN SEEMINGLY WOULD WIN THE FIGHT. PAUL CAME TO THE CONCLUSION HE NEEDED JESUS AND THE POWER OF HIS SPIRIT TO GIVE HIM THE VICTORY OVER HIS FLESHLY NATURE. IN GALATIANS 5: 17 "FOR THE FLESH LUSTETH AGAINST THE SPIRIT AND THE SPIRIT AGAINST THE FLESH; AND THESE ARE CONTRARY THE ONE TO THE OTHER; SO THAT WE CANNOT DO THE THINGS THAT YE WOULD".

THEREFORE, IT IS REASONABLE TO CONSIDER THAT WHICHEVER ONE IS FED THE MOST, USUALLY IS THE STRONGER. WE LOVE THE COSMETICS OF CHRISTIANITY MORE THAN THE NATURE OF CHRISTIANITY. WE LOVE THE SUPERFICIAL AND WHAT PEOPLE SEE ON THE OUTSIDE MORE THAN WHAT THEY CAN SEE ON THE INSIDE. SUPERFICIAL ON THE OUTSIDE, BUT DEAD ON THE INSIDE. LOOKING GOOD ON CHURCH ATTENDANCE BUT DEAD-ON FELLOWSHIP; LOOKING GOOD ON PRAISING THE LORD, BUT DEAD ON GIVING TO THE LORD; LOOKING GOOD AND FEEDING THE SUPERFICIAL MAN BUT DEAD ON FEEDING THE SPIRITUAL MAN.

DRESSED UP AND LOOKING GOOD ON SUNDAY BUT DEAD TO LETTING YOUR LIGHT OF GOD SHINE ON MONDAY; DRESSED UP AND OUTSIDE; BUT DEAD TO FORGIVENESS, DEAD TO KINDNESS, DEAD TO LOVE COVERING A MULTITUDE OF FAULTS. LIVING WITH A PURPOSE. KNOW THIS SATAN HAS NO PLANS ON GIVING UP AND GOD WILL NOT SURRENDER, SATAN HAS SOME POWER, BUT GOD HAS ALL THE POWER. FEED THE SPIRITUAL MAN AND BECOME A SERVANT OF GOD. ONLY SECURE SUBMISSIVE PEOPLE IN THE SPIRIT OF GOD END UP BEING GOOD SERVANTS OF GOD. PAUL ENCOURAGED TIMOTHY TO LIVE WITH A PURPOSE; 2 TIM. 2: 1-5. SERVANT PEOPLE OF GOD DON'T WORRY ABOUT PRESTIGE, SERVANT PEOPLE OF GOD ARE NOT CONCERNED WITH POWER, SERVANT PEOPLE OF GOD ARE NOT CONCERNED WITH POPULARITY. SERVANT PEOPLE OF GOD ARE CONCERNED WITH HOW THEY CAN PLEASE THEIR MASTER JESUS CHRIST AND THEREFORE CONSTANTLY FEED THE SPIRIT OF MAN SO THEY MAY WIN THE FIGHT OF FAITH. ONLY SERVANTS OF GOD END UP BEING GREAT IN THE KINGDOM. JESUS SAID IF ANY OF YOU WILL BECOME GREAT, LET HIM FIRST BECOME A SERVANT.

ROMANS 6:16-19. "KNOW YE NOT THAT TO WHOM YE YIELD YOURSELVES SERVANTS TO OBEY, HIS SERVANTS YE ARE TO WHOM YE OBEY; WHETHER OF SIN UNTO DEATH, OR OF OBEDIENCE UNTO RIGHTEOUSNESS? BUT GOD BE THANKED, THAT YE WERE THE SERVANTS OF SIN, BUT YE HAVE OBEYED FROM THE HEART THAT FORM OF DOCTRINE WHICH WAS DELIVERED UNTO YOU. BEING THEN MADE FREE FROM SIN, YE BECAME THE SERVANTS OF RIGHTEOUSNESS". LIVING WITH A PURPOSE -TWO NATURES IN US – CHOOSE THE SPIRITUAL NATURE.

MINISTER PAUL SANDERS, SMITHSONIA
CHURCH OF CHRIST,

# IF GOD AUTHORIZE IT, HE WILL CERTAINLY RECOGNIZE IT.

**Allow What You See
To Hinder What**

Father we thank you now for what you are about to do in this place. One day you Jesus took Peter, James, and John up into a high mountain and while they were there appeared unto them Moses and Elias talk with him. Peter spoke boldly and said, "Lord, it is good for us to be here", not knowing why he was there. But while he was talking there was a transformation taking place.

I do declare today there might be someone here today that might not know why they are here; but I do declare today that there is a transformation that is about to take place in their life.

God's word said in Matt 17:1-5, "behold a bright cloud over shadowing them which indicate that it was the Spirit of God, which represents life and out of the cloud a voice spoke and said "This is my beloved Son, in whom I am well pleased; hear ye him." And when the disciples heard it, they fell on their face and were sore afraid. Jesus said Arise, be not afraid.

No man come unto the Father except the Spirit draws them and I pray

Paul Sanders, Smithsonia Church of Christ, Florence, AL that you will kill my flesh so that the Spirit of God will arise that they may hear ye him. I decrease that he may increase. I will sit down that he may stand up. Now Father I pray that you will bless the place. Destroy every yoke, heal every pain mentally, physically and
spiritually in the name of Jesus. That was THEN and this is NOW. And we thank you now Father for the Spirit to Overcome. Father I pray it now in Jesus name. Now finally, Father let the words of my mouth and the meditation of my heart be acceptable in thy sight O Lord my Strength and my Redeemer it is in Jesus Magnificent, Glorious, Marvelous, Holy, Awesome name we pray, Amen. Come on Clap those Hands and give the Lord some praise! He is so worthy. He is from Everlasting to Everlasting; He is the First and the Last; He is the Beginning and the End. If you came into this world by God then you need to leave out with God. Job said naked I came into this world and naked I shall return the Lord gave and the Lord take it away Bless be the name of the Lord. Though he slay me, yet will I trust
him. Now, somebody today that is not ashamed (Shout Out ONLY) and that is Only what you do for Christ will last. Somebody give him PRAISE! Somebody give him GLORY!

Paul Sanders, Smithsonia Church of Christ, Florence, AL If you are not so mean tonight and if you are a child of the King would you look at two or three people and prophesy to them these words. Dont' Allow What You See To Hinder What You Believe. I do declare tonight that in the body of Christ there are
some people that have CRAZY FAITH. No matter what the Doctor have said No matter what the enemy have said No matter what your best friend have said
No matter what your employer have said No matter what your bank account shows and as a matter of fact no matter what the banker have said That you are not going to Allow What You See To Hinder What You Believe. Now that is a good place to give GOD some praise. If you know that he is going to bring you through, then you have to learn how to THANK HIM in ADVANCE. Thank him for what he has done already, Thank him for what he is getting ready to do in your life. Thank him for the seasons that you are in now & Thank him for the seasons to come in Jesus name. Come on let us celebrate him now with a Hallelujah praise! Paul Sanders, Smith sonia Church of Christ, Florence, AL In the book of Genesis Israel was born.

AND AS A MATTER OF FACT THERE IS NO TIME TO WONDER ABOUT IT OR WORRY ABOUT IT YOU WERE BORN AND YOU ARE AS REAL AS IT GET. COME ON, YOU KNOW WHAT I AM TALKING ABOUT THE OLD MAN THAT CAME OUT OF YOU. BUT... GOD HAS ALLOWED YOU TO BE BORN IN A SEASON THAT WAS RIPE FOR HARVEST, BUT NOW HE IS LOOKING FOR LABORS. GOD IS NOT SO MUCH CONCERN ABOUT YOUR PHYSICAL MAN BECAUSE YOU ARE ALREADY HERE. BUT THERE IS ANOTHER SIDED OF YOU THAT GOD IS CONCERN ABOUT AND THAT IS THE SPIRITUAL SIDE OF YOU THAT GOD IS READY TO BIRTH AND BRING FORTH AND WAKE UP THAT SPIRITUAL MAN THAT MAYBE STILL SLEEPING IN SIDE OF YOU. JESUS TELL NICODEMUS IN (JOHN 3:6-7): "THAT WHICH IS BORN OF THE FLESH IS FLESH AND THAT WHICH IS BORN OF THE SPIRIT IS SPIRIT. MARVEL NOT THAT I SAID UNTO THEE, YE MUST BE BORN AGAIN."

YES, ISRAEL WAS BORN, BUT GOD WAS NOT JUST CONCERN ABOUT THEIR PHYSICAL MAN HE WANTED TO TEACH THEM ABOUT THE SPIRITUAL SIDE OF HIM. ***IN THE BOOK OF EXODUS ISRAEL WAS CHOSEN. AND NOW IN (ROMANS 2:10-11): THE WORD SAID, "BUT GLORY, HONOUR, AND PEACE, TO EVERY MAN THAT WORKETH GOOD, TO PAUL SANDERS, SMITHSONIA CHURCH OF CHRIST, FLORENCE, AL THE JEW FIRST, AND ALSO TO THE GEN'-TILE: FOR THERE IS NO RESPECT OF PERSONS WITH GOD."

ANYONE OF YOU CAN BE CHOSEN BY GOD TO DO WHATEVER PLAN THAT GOD HAS FOR YOUR LIFE. GOD SAID IN (JEREMIAH 29:11) – "FOR I KNOW THE THOUGHTS THAT I THINK TOWARD YOU, SAITH THE LORD, THOUGHTS OF PEACE, AND NOT OF EVIL, TO GIVE YOU AN EXPECTED END." GOD HAS ALLOWED ME TO COME TO TELL YOU "DON'T ALLOW WHAT YOU SEE TO HINDER WHAT YOU BELIEVE."

THE KEY WORD IN THE BOOK OF JOSHUA IS POSSESSION. GOD HAD GIVEN THE CHILDREN OF ISRAEL THEIR LAND IN AN UNCONDITIONAL COVENANT. IN (GENESIS 17:8) GOD SAID TO

ARBAHAM "AND I WILL GIVE UNTO THEE, AND TO THY SEED AFTER THEE, THE LAND WHEREIN THOU ART A STRANGER, ALL THE LAND OF CANAAN, FOR AN EVERLASTING POSSESSION; AND I WILL BE THEIR GOD". HOWEVER, ISRAEL'S POSSESSION OF THE LAND WAS CONDITIONAL. THERE WAS CONFLICT AND THERE WAS CONQUEST. THEY HAD TO FIGHT BATTLES AND LAY HOLD OF THEIR POSSESSIONS.

HOW MANY OF YOU KNOW TONIGHT THAT YOU HAVE TO FIGHT FOR WHAT IS RIGHT; NOT PHYSICALLY BUT SPIRITUALLY.

PAUL SANDERS, SMITHSONIA CHURCH OF CHRIST, FLORENCE, AL THE APOSTLE PAUL SAYS IT LIKE THIS IN (2 CORINTHIANS 10:4) – "FOR THE WEAPONS OF OUR WARFARE ARE NOT CARNAL, BUT MIGHTY THROUGH GOD TO THE PULLING DOWN OF STRONG HOLDS CASTING DOWN EVERY IMAGINATION AND EVERY HIGH THING THAT HAS EXALTED ITSELF AGAINST THE KNOWLEDGE OF CHRIST. BRINGING INTO CAPTIVITY EVERY THOUGHT UNTO THE OBEDIENCE OF CHRIST"

***I do declare that there is something that has come against you in the natural to hinder you in the

Spiritual. But today, Somebody Shout out TODAY! "You Are Not Going To Allow What You See To

Hinder What You Believe."

As we move to our Text: (Joshua Chapter 1:1-2) : "Now after the death of Moses the servant of the Lord it came to pass, that the Lord spake unto Joshua the son of Nun, Moses' minister, saying

Moses my servant is dead; now therefore arise, go over this Jordan, thou, and all this people, unto the land which I do give to, even to the children of Israel."

## THERE IS ONE THINGIN THE TEXT THAT I WANT TO POINT OUT TO YOU ON WHAT TO DO WHEN YOU ARE HINDERED

1. The First thing that you should do when you are hinder is - (NOT TO SIT STILL) – Verse 2 -- Mo'- Paul Sanders, Smithsonia Church of Christ, Florence, AL see my servant is dead. Now therefore arise, go over this Jor'-dan, thou, and all this people, unto the land which I do give to them, even to the children of Is'-ra-el. It was a sad day in the camp. The people mourn for Moses 30 days. And God now is saying to Joshua. As a reminder. Moses my servant is dead. What do you do when a leader or a love one has passed. Do you still have thirty days of mourning or do you have a celebration because God work must still go on. Joshua I only allow Moses to be with you for a certain season. Now it is time for you to obey what I have started with Moses.

 And God said to Joshua Now therefore arise, go over this Jordan, thou, and all this people, unto the land which I do give to them, even to the children of Is'-ra-el. And the Lord is saying to the City of Zion tonight and to all those that are here. That God is getting ready to bring you into your destiny.

Don't allow what you see to hinder what you believe. The EYE is a very vital part of the body. And sometimes when you look to long you will begin to look

wrong. Paul Sanders, Smithsonia Church of Christ, Florence, AL I do declare that there are things that come to hinder your walk with the Lord. Well what do you see that comes to hinder you.

1. Old Dead Relationship will start creeping back in.
2. When people call you everything but a child of God.
3. When the deck is stack up against you and you don't know what to do.

Well what do you believe? I believe: No weapon that is formed against thee shall prosper; and every tongue that shall rise against thee in judgment thou shall condemn. (Isaiah 54:17) I believe: Greater is he that is in you, than he that is in the world (I John 4:4). I believe: But my God shall supply all your need according to his riches in glory by Christ Je'-sus.

(Philippians 3:19)

 I believe: I can do all things through Christ which strengthened me. (Philippians 3:13) I believe: I will lift up my eyes unto the hill, from whence cometh my help. My help come the from the Lord, which made heaven and earth (Psalm 121). I believe: The Lord is my Shepard I shall not want he make me to lie down in green pastures: he leadeth me beside the still waters.

He restoreth my soul: he leadeth me in the paths of righteousness for his name's sake Paul Sanders, Smithsonia Church of Christ, Florence, AL Yea, thou I walk through the valley of the shadow of death, I will fear no evil: for thou art with me; thy rod and thy staff they comfort me. Thou preparest a table before me in the presence of mine enemies: thou anointest my head with oil; my cup runneth over. Surely goodness and mercy shall follow me all the days of my life: and I will dwell in the house of the LORD forever.

# MINISTER LUKE MYLES

From Chicago Illinois

## Forgiveness

Many times life presents us with an immense amount of tantalizing and chaotic encounters. We may find ourselves in pursuit of the unattainable, disregarding the supernatural assistance we have access to via Jehovah Ezrah ("Lord, our help"). We are in dire need of repentance and restoration due to our innate sinful nature that separates us from the Creator.

Repentance is the act of forsaking and turning from the transgressions committed against the laws of The Most High God. 1 John 3:4 tells us that anyone who makes a practice of sinning also practices lawlessness. In the Bible, those who do not know Christ are called "workers of lawlessness". Unbelievers are marked by lawlessness.

The Hebrew word pesha refers to ways that people violate the trust of others. Pesha describes the betrayal of a relationship. Since there are many kinds of relationships, a lot of different behaviors can be called pesha.

Our human nature does battle with the idea of forgiving those who have hurt us. Human beings can truly commit grossly indecent and flat out horrible acts against each other. Some atrocities are difficult to describe, or to think about, let alone forgiving someone who has done them. All the same, Jesus insists we understand how much God has forgiven us. The parable in Matthew 18:21-35 explains that we have all sinned against God, and by comparison, our sin against our Creator is far more than any person can sin against another.

As believers, we are constantly engaged in spiritual warfare. In Ephesians 6, Apostle Paul affirms that our battle is indeed spiritual, not physical. The enemies we face, ultimately, are not people or objects. The devil may use those as apart of his attacks, but our true opponent is not other people. Forgiveness is a choice. When we choose not to forgive, we have now given the enemy an open door to creep in and wreak havoc via our unforgiving spirit. Once he's in, he'll bombard our hearts and minds with spirits of bitterness, stubbornness ,pride,infirmities, and most commonly: stress. Will not stress kill us?! Yes! John 10:10 reminds us that the enemy's job is to kill, steal, and destroy. His job is to wear us out! Shall we allow the enemy to make a mess of our lives because we're too prideful to forgive?

Since this is a battle, we must fight to forgive. Fighting is defined as taking part in a violent struggle by the use of weapons. Our weapons of defense are prayer, fasting, the blood of Jesus, and praise. Praise? Yes! Imagine the devil sending someone to betray you to gain access to your mind and your first response is praise? Yes it is easier said than done but even during a time of betrayal (when you are at your weakest), praise is necessary. Confuse the enemy. Make him mad. James told us to count it all joy when we encounter various trials. We must break our patterns of unforgiveness with obedience and praise. As believers,it's not an option. Petition the help of Jesus Christ to replace our stony,stubborn hearts with hearts of flesh. (Ezekiel 36:26)
Amid this battle,our greatest weapon of defense is the blood of Jesus Christ. It'll behoove us to use his blood as if it were bleach. Ask the Lord to sanitize our minds,hearts, and bodies. Implore the Lord to sanitize the entire situation and make it as if it never happened. Can not the Creator of the universe make this so?

Many believers (and nonbelievers) have made it a custom to declare their forgiveness without forgetting the transgressions committed against them. If forgiveness means to completely let go of resentment, why then should we keep an account of the transgression if we've claimed forgiveness? Utterly preposterous! Imagine sincerely repenting of our various sins and being forgiven by God but still being reminded by him of the things we've done. Did not the Lord declare in Hebrews 10:17 "their sins and iniquities will I remember no more"? Who,then, do we think we are to forgive but not forget?

Repentance is nonnegotiable concerning aligning (or realigning) ourselves with and returning back to the fold of God. Restoration requires the hearing and belief of God's word. Forsaking one's sinful life is also of the utmost importance when seeking restoration. In Luke 13:1- 5, Jesus expounds on his lesson he had just taught. In Luke 12:57-59, Jesus told the crowd to reconcile with other people they have wronged. In Luke 13:5, he repeats his warning with urgency. He gives us a fair warning to reconcile with one another quickly. Death comes to everyone and sometimes that death is sudden and unfair. This serves as a testament to the importance of forgiveness, repentance, and reconciliation with God NOW.

We have a limited amount of time on earth, and we don't know when it will end. Not everyone gets the chance to have a "deathbed conversion". It is far better to take advantage of the time we have, confess our sins, accept Jesus as our Savior, and ensure we will live for eternity with the Creator. Forgiveness may be defined as the act of no longer holding a guilty charge against one who has trespassed against you, pardoning/ canceling a debt, and releasing resentment or anger. Considering our prideful spirits, many times as believers we adopt the notion that forgiveness is optional, but it is not.

In Matthew 6:15, Jesus explicitly states that those who refuse to forgive others will not be forgiven for their own sins by God. Take time to imagine how innately sinful we are as humans. We sin against our father daily, yet if we're sincere in asking for his forgiveness, are not we fully confident that we will be forgiven instantly?

Hebrews 10:17 "their sins and iniquities will I remember no more"? Who,then, do we think we are to forgive but not forget?

The Bible also teaches us in 1 Corinthians 13:5 that unselfish love is the basis for true forgiveness since it keeps no record of wrongs. Is forgiveness as easy as it seems? Absolutely not. If it is our goal to truly walk with the Lord, it is imperative to feast on his word, and his instructions for us. With the guidance of the greatest assistant we could ever ask for, The Holy Spirit, all things are possible and can be done so in a supernatural way if only we believe. Forgiveness will never work if total restoration isn't implemented. The biblical meaning of the word restoration is to receive back more than has been lost to the point where the final state is greater than the original condition. With the help of The Most High God, anything is possible if only we are willing to dismantle our stubborn and prideful heart. Shall we continue to give the enemy an open door to wreak havoc in our lives and jeopardize seeing our Savior's face in peace?

# Within the stillness of your soul lies the infinite light of the universe, guiding you toward peace and purpose.

# Minister Eddie Jones

**87th, ST, Church Of Christ**

# THE THANKFULNESS OF PRAYER/THE POWER OF PRAYER

EPHESIANS 6:10-18
THE POWER OF PRAYER.
I HAVE BEEN STUDYING FOR THE LAST FEW WEEKS IN THE BOOK OF EPHESIANS. OUTFITTING FOR THE BATTLE MAKING READY TO DO SPIRITUAL WARFARE WITH THE DEVIL , FOR THE SCRIPTURE SAYS THAT WE DO NOT WRESTLE AGAINST FLESH AND BLOOD, BUT AGAINST PRINCIPALITIES, AGAINST POWERS,AGAINST THE DARKNESS OF THIS AGE AGAINST SPIRITUAL WICKEDNESS, IN HIGH PLACES. AND SO IF WE ARE GOING TO BE VICTORIOUS IN THE BATTLE IF WE ARE GOING TO BE INGAGE AND ENJOINED IN THE BATTLE. THEN THE SCRIPTURES SAYS THERE SOMETHINGS WE NEED TO PUT ON AND KEEP ON AND THEN THERE ARE SOME WEAPONS WE OUGHT TO TAKE UP. WE OUGHT TO PUT ON THE GRIDDLE OF TRUTH..WE OUGHT TO PUT ON THE BREAST PLATE OF  RIGHTEOUSNESS....WE OUGHT TO HAVE OUR FEET FITTED WITH THE PREPARATION OF THE GOSPEL OF PEACE .....BUT WE MUST TAKE UP THE SHEILD OF FAITH.......WE GOT TO TAKE THE HELMET OF SALVATION .....AND THEN WE GOT TO TAKE THE SWORD OF THE SPIRIT......WHICH IS THE WORD OF GOD....THE ONLY WAY YOU CAN BE VICTORIOUS IN WARFARE AGAINST THE DEVIL IS YOU GOT TO BE FAMILIAR INTIMATELY WITH THE WORD OF GOD.

DEMONS TREMBLE AT THE SOUND OF HIS NAME. STRONG HOLDS ARE BROKEN WHEN WE ENJOINED THE WORD OF GOD, BECAUSE WE HAVE NO POWER OF OURSELVES BUT THE POWER IS IN THE WORD OF GOD. SO NOW AS WE MOVE THROUGH EPHESIANS, WRAPPING UP THE OUTFIT FOR THE BATTLE, EVERYTHING WE NEED TO DO, WHILE WE BATTLE WITH THE DEVIL HAS BEEN GIVEN TO TO US IN THE SCRIPTURE IN THE WORD OF GOD AND HERE IS WHAT WE NEED FINALLY TO BE VICTORIOUS OVER THE DEVIL. WE NEED THE POWER OF PRAYER. BECAUSE A GRIDLE OF TRUTH, A BREAST PLATE OF RIGHTEOUSNESS, A SWORD OF THE SPIRIT, A HELMET OF SALVATION, THE SHIELD OF FAITH AND SHOES OF THE GOSPLE OF PEACE WITHOUT PRAYER IS INEFFECTIVE. WE NEED POWERFUL PRAYER. FERVENT PRAYER, HONEST PRAYER, SPECIFIC PRAYER, JUST PRAYER, YOU GOT TO MOVE IN YOUR PRAYER LIFE FROM GENERALITY TO SPECIFICITY. YOU HAVE TO BE READY TO TELL GOD WHAT IT IS THAT YOU SPECIFICALLY WANT HIM TO DO ABOUT A PARTICULAR SITUATION IN YOUR LIFE, BECAUSE PRAYER WILL HELP YOU TO STAND AGAINST THE WILDS OF THE DEVIL. LET ME SEE IF I CAN GIVE YOU MY WORKING DEFINITION OF PRAYER, I HAD TO THINK ABOUT IT FOR WHILE AND AS I TOLD YOU BEFORE I COME FROM A PRAYING

FAMILY......................AND I HAVE GIVEN THIS SOME THOUGHT NOW FOR SOME OF YOU, YOU MAY GET THIS RIGHT AWAY, IT TOOK ME A WHILE CHURCH, "PRAYER IS EARTH GIVEN HEAVEN PERMISSION TO INTER FEAR IN HER AFFAIRS" I DIDN'T GET IT RIGHT AWAY, I'M SLOW BUT PRAYER IS EARTH GIVING HEAVEN PERMISSION TO INTERFERE.

I HAD TO CHEW ON THAT A MINUTE. BECAUSE I NEVER THOUGHT HEAVEN, GOD NEEDING PERMISSION TO DO ANYTHING.BUT WHEN I GAVE IT ANOTHER LOOK, GOD GAVE US DOMINION TO RULE OVER THE EARTH AND SINCE WE HAVE DOMINION TO RULE OVER THE EARTH, GOD HAS GIVING US FREEDOM THAT WE CAN LET HIM COME IN AND HELP US RULE OR WE CAN SHUT HIM OUT. BUT IF WE NEED HIS HELP, WE GOT ASK HIM FOR IT. SOMEBODY GONE TO GET IT.

CHURCH GOD KNOWS WHAT YOUR STORMS, GOD KNOWS YOUR STORY HE KNOWS IF YOU ARE FAKE, FLIMSY, FOOLISH OR FRAGILE. GOD KNOWS WHAT YOU ARE GOING THRU. GOD KNOWS WHAT YOU ARE UP AGAINST, BUT GOD WILL NOT GET INVOLVED IN IT UNTIL YOU ASK HIM. ASK AND IT SHALL BE GIVEN, SEEK AND YE SHALL FIND, KNOCK AND THE DOOR WILL BE OPEN. GOD WILL COME TO YOUR RESCUE AND HAS COME TO ALL OF OUR STORMS IT MAY HAVE NOT BEEN THE WAY, YOU WANTED IT BUT HE BROUGHT YOU THRU. LEND ME YOUR BIBLICAL MINDS FOR JUST A MINTUE. HE SAW ADAM AND EVE IN THE GARDEN WALKING NAKED AND HE CAME AND SPOKE TO THEM LIKE HE USUSAL DID AND HE CALL OUT TO THEM WHERE ARE YOU ADAM? ADAM SAID I WAS HIDING BECAUSE I WAS NAKED. GOD SAID YOU VE BEEN NAKED, WHO TOLD YOU THAT YOU WERE NAKED? AND THEN ADAM STARTED DOING WHAT WE STILL DO HE SHIFTED THE BLAME "THAT WOMEN YOU GAVE ME" AND THAT'S ANOTHER SERMON. AND THEN THE WOMEN SAID THE DEVIL MADE ME DO IT" AND IT WASN'T UNTIL ADAM AND EVE BECAME HONEST WITH GOD THAT GOD REMEDIED THEIR SIN SITUATION. THEY SEWED FIG LEAVES TOGETHER which WAS AN INADEQUATE COVERING BUT THEN GOD SACRIFICED AN ANIMAL AND PUT SKINS ON THAT ANIMAL AND SHED BLOOD FOR WITHOUT THE SHEDDING OF BLOOD THERE IS NO REMISSION OF SIN.THOES DISCIPLES THAT WERE ON THAT SHIP AND A STORM BLEW UP JESUS KNEW THEY WERE IN TROUBLE.

BECAUSE HE WAS ON THE BOAT WITH THEM AND THE BIBLE SAYS THAT HE WAS SO CONFIDENT ABOUT WHO HE WAS, THAT IN THE STORM HE'S ASLEEP ON APILLOW AND IT WAS NOT UNTIL THEY RECOGNIZES THEY COULD NOT HANDLE IT THAT JESUS GOT UP. IT WAS NOT UNTIL SOMEONE SAID MASTER DON'T YOU CARE THAT WE ARE ABOUT TO PERISH? THAT'S A CRY FOR HELP AND WHEN THEY CRIED OUT JESUS GOT ON THE BOWE OF THAT SHIP AND SHAID "PEACE BE STILL" THE STORM WOULD STILL BE RAGING IF THEY DIDN'T CRY OUT. REMEMBER ANOTHER OCCASION WHEN THEY WERE ON THE SEA OF GALILEE AND JESUS WAS IN THE HILLS IN THE MOUNTAIN PRAYING AND A STORM BLEW UP AND IT'S ABOUT 4 AM IN THE MORNING AND THEY DON'T SEE HIM BUT HE SEES THEM AND THE BIBLE SAYS HE COMES WALKING ON THE WATER AND THE GOSPEL OF MARK SAYS AND HE WOULD HAVE PASSES THEM BYE BUT SOMEBODY CRYED OUT AND TODAY THE LORD JESUS IS HERE AND READY TO HELP WITH YOUR STORM BUT YOU MUST CRY OUT OR he WILL PASS YOU BYE. I'VE LEARNED YOU CAN'T DO IT BY YOURSELF YOU CAN'T HANDLE THESE BURDENS ALONE. LET JESUS BEAR YOUR CROSS SO THAT THE WORLD WHO LOST CAN SEE WHAT JESUS HAS DONE IN YOUR LIFE. WHEN YOU NEED THE LORD BAD ENOUGH, WHEN YOUR SITUATION BECOMES DESPERATE ENOUGH YOU DON'T CARE WHO'S LOOKING AT YOU, YOU DON'T CARE WHOES SITTING NEXT TO YOU, YOU ARE NOT BOTHER ABOUT WHO'S TALKING ABOUT YOU, WHO SEES YOU CRYING, " FATHER I STRECH MY HANDS TO THEE & quot;

NOW YOU CAN SET HERE AND ACT LIKE YOU DON'T KNOW HIM IF YOU WANT TOO, BUT YOUR SITUATION HAS NOT GOT DESPERATE YET, YOU HAVEN'T GOTTEN DOWN TO YOUR LAST DIME YET, YOU HAVEN'T BEEN SICK ENOUGH YET, YOU HAVEN'T CRIED IN THE MIDNIGHT ENOUGH YET, BUT WHEN YOU GET TOO WHERE YOU CAN'T HANDLE IT, HE WILL HELP YOU BUT YOU WILL HAVE TO ASK I WANT YOU TO LOOK WITH ME FOR A MOMENT AT THE MANY PHASIC OF PRAYER THAT PAUL SHARES WITH US IN EPHESIANS. THERE FIRST OF ALL IS A VARIETIES OF PRAYERS. ITS IN VERSE NUMBER 18, HE SAYS PRAYING ALWAYS WITH ALL PRAYER AND SUPPLICATION. WITH ALL PRAYER AND SUPPLICATION, TO USE BOTH OF THESE WORDS POINTS TO THE IDEA THAT WE OUGHT TO BE INVOLVED IN ALL KINDS OF PRAYER. PRAY WHEN YOU SET DOWN TO EAT YOUR FOOD, PRAY WHEN YOU ARE ON THE EXPRESSWAYS, PRAY WHEN YOU AT YOUR DESK AT WORK, PRAY WHEN YOU ARE AT HOME WASHING AND DRYING CLOTHES, PRAY WHEN YOU ARE JOGGING ON THE THE TRED MILL, PRAY WHEN YOU ARE SETTING DOWN NEXT TO SOMEONE WHO WANT SPEAK TO YOU,
PRAY FOR YOUR ENEMIES,
PRAY FOR YOUR FRIENDS,
PRAY FOR YOUR HUSBAND,
PRAY FOR YOUR CHILDREN,
PRAY FOR YOUR WIFE,
PRAY FOR IN YOUR INLAW'S,
PRAY FOR YOUR CO WORKERS,

PRAY FOR THE DOPE DEALER,
PRAY FOR THE POOR CHILD WHOS MOM AND DAD WANT COME HOME,
PRAY FOR THE PRESIDENT,
PRAY FOR THE PO PO,
PRAY FOR THE JUDGES,
PRAY FOR THE CHURCH, PRAY PRAY PRAY PRAY PRAY PRAY PRAY,
PRAY ALL THE TIME, AND FOR THAT PERSON WHO THINKS THEY KNOW ALL AND
SAYS YOU DON'T HAVE TO PRAY THAT MUCH, MY BIBLE SAYS PRAY IN SEASON
AND OUT OF SEASON AND YOU DON'T HAVE TO BE ON YOUR KNEES TO PRAY.
BECAUSE SOMETIMES WHEN YOU GET IN TROUBLE, YOU DON'T HAVE TIME TO
,
GET SOMEPLACE BY YOURSELF. WHEREVER YOU YOU ARE. SOMETIMES YOU
DON'T Have A MINUTE TO CLOSE YOUR EYES,
YOU JUST HAVE TO PRAY WITH YOUR EYES OPEN.
SOMETIMES YOU DON'T HAVE TIME FOR A LONG DROWN OUT PRAYER
YOU ARE IN TROUBLE "FATHER, I NEED YOU TO COME RIGHT AWAY I AM
WALKING
IN THIS DOCTORS OFFICE AND I DON'T KNOW WHY HE CALLED ME HERE. I
DON'T KNOW WHAT
TEST RESULT WILL SHOW, BUT I KNOW YOU AND I KNOW WHAT YOU HAVE DONE FOR
ME BEFORE,
SO, I'M PUTTING IT IN YOUR HANDS.
ANYBODY HERE EVER BEEN THERE?
GOD I'M DOWN TO MY LAST $20, I DON'T WANT
TO ASK ANYBODY BECAUSE I DON'T WANT THEM TALKING AND GOSSIPING
ABOUT ME. I NEED YOU TO MAKE A WAY OUT OF NO WAY.
AND WATCH THE LORD SEND YOU A BLESSING.
BECAUSE WHEN YOU PRAY ALL THE TIME YOU DON'T HAVE TO PRAY LONG
YOU DON'T HAVE TO PRAY LOUD YOU DON'T EVEN HAVE TO OPEN YOUR
MOUTH
TO PRAY WHEN YOU SETTING DOWN TO TALK TO YOUR SUPERVISOR BECAUSE
SOMEONE AT YOUR JOB IS TRYING TO GET YOU FIRED. AND WATCH GOD WORK IT
OUT.
YOU CAN PRAY ON YOUR WAY TO THE BANK AND WHEN YOU SET DOWN TO
FEEL OUT THAT LOAN APPLICATION, GOD HAS ALREADY WORKED IT OUT.
BECAUSE PRAYER THAT WORKS,
IT'S NOT MAGIC,
IT IS NOT VODOO,

PRAYER, IS YOU ASKING GOD TO INTERFERE IN YOUR SITUATION.
GOD, I CAN'T DO IT UNLESS YOU PUT YOUR HANDS ON IT,
GOD, I HAVE RAISED THIS CHILD THE BEST I KNOW HOW, NOW I PUT
HIM OR HER IN YOUR HANDS. HAVE YOU EVER HEARD A MOTHERS CRY OUT FOR
CHILD? I DON'T know WHAT I GOING TO DO HE WANT LISTEN, HE WANT
OBEY.
LORD, I GET DOWN ON MY KNEES, A PRAY FOR HIS PROTECTION.
THERE ARE SOME MOTHERS HERE THAT HAVE SAID THOES VERY WORDS.
BECAUSE CHRUCH SOMEBODY PRAYED FOR ME. I WISH I HAD A HAD WITNESS
TODAY.
BECAUSE I'M WHERE I AM TODAY A SHEPHERD, BECAUSE SOMEBODY
PRAYED
FOR ME, I SHOULD HAVE BEEN DEAD, I COULD HAVE BEEN IN THE PENITENTIARY,
BUT SOMEBODY PRAYED FOR ME. AND YOU OUGHT TO THANK GOD RIGHT
WHERE YOU ARE SITTING NOW THAT SOMEBODY LOVED YOU ENOUGH TO
PRAY FOR YOU.
SAINTS OF GOD, I NEED TO LOOK AT THE FREQUENCY OF PRAYER
THE BIBLE SAYS PRAY ALL THE TIME.
CHRUCH, WE NEED TO LEARN HOW TO BE IN AN ATTITUDE TO PRAY.
IN AN CONTINUAL GOD CONCISENESS. THAT WHEN YOU SEE SOMETHING
BEAUTIFUL, SOMETHING ALL INSPIRING, SOMETHING THAT JUST MOVES YOU,
YOU SAY GOD THANK FOR THAT WHEN YOU SEE A NEW BORN BABY, WHEN
YOU WITNESS A SUN SET OR SUN RISE OR WHEN YOU SEE GOD WORK OUT A
SITUATION THAT SEEM IMPOSSIBLE. YOU OUGHT TO SAY GOD THANK YOU FOR
THAT.
OR WHEN YOU SEE EVIL TAKEN PLACE YOU OUGHT TO PRAY GOD PLEASE DO
SOMETHING ABOUT THAT SITUATION. SOME WIVES, SOME CHILD BEING ABUSED,
TALK TO GOD AND ASK HIM TO HANDLE THAT SITUATION. AND THOSE KINDS Of
Prayer

THE FREQUENCY OF YOUR PRAYERS MOVES GOD TO INTERFERE.
WITH EVERYTHING WE SEE AND EVERYTHING WE EXPERIENCE, BECOMES A KIND
OF SILENT PRAYER. THANK GOD WHEN YOU GET UP IN THE MORNING,
THANK GOD YOU ABLE TO GET UP IN THE MORNING. YOUR KNEE IS HURTING
YOUR HIP IS BOTHERING YOU BUT THANK GOD YOU CAN STILL FEEL SOMETHING.
YOU FORGET WHERE YOU PUT YOUR EYEGLASSES, BUT THANK GOD YOU CAN
STILL
SEE, EVERYTHING YOU WANT TO REMEMBER, YOU GOT TO WRITE IT DOWN
AND SOMETIMES YOU YOU HAVE TO REMEMBER WHAT YOU WROTE IT ON.
BUT THANK GOD YOU ARE STILL IN YOUR RIGHT MIND. HAVE I GOT A WITNESS.
THANK GOD FOR 60'S,70'S, 80'S WAIT, 50'S, 40'S,
30' AND 20'S.

BECAUSE WE ARE STILL ABLE TO GET AROUND,
AND STILL ABLE TO COME TO CHURCH AND LOOK BACK OVER WHERE YOU VE COME
FROM AND THANK GOD FOR HOW GOOD HE'S BEEN TO YOU, EVERY TIME YOU
THINK ABOUT IT YOU OUGHT TO TELL GOD THANK YOU.
NOW I NEED SOMEBODY RIGHT HERE WHO HAS SOMETHING TO BE GRATEFUL FOR
YOU DON'T HAVE TO TELL ME OR THE
PERSON NEXT TO YOU, BUT GOD KNOWS WHAT YOU VE BEEN THROUGH AND WHAT
HE'S BROUGHT YOU THROUGH.
IT'S THANKING TIME, THANK GOD FOR YOUR STORMS,
THANK GOD FOR YOUR TEARS,
THANK GOD FOR YOUR SCARS, BECAUSE, THEY MADE YOU WHO YOU ARE .
YOU WOULD NOT BE THE STRONG PERSON OF FAITH, IF GOD HAD NOT BROUGHT YOU THROUGH.
YOU WOULD NOT HAVE THE TESTIMONY THAT YOU HAVE NOW,

IF GOD HAD NOT BEEN GOOD TO YOU AND DELIVER YOU, WHEN HE SHOULD HAVE LET YOU FALL
IS THERE ANYBODY HERE THAT THE LOVES THE LORD,
IS THERE ANYBODY HERE TODAY THAT KNOWS IT WAS GODS HAND THAT KEEP FROM FALLING.
THEN A & quote; THANK YOU LORD& quote; IS IN ORDER.
YOUNG PEOPLE LEARN HOW TO PUT PRAYER ON YOUR AGENDA......
AMEN

CHURCH OF CHRIST
At 10:30 A.M.
87th Street Church of Christ
Sunday, May 19, 2024
Sermon Presentation
Fixing Life's Hanging Slips!
Luke 22:31-32, 55-62

It's A Family Affair!
Friends And Family Day
at the
87th St. Church of Christ

From The State Of Georgia
Dr. Torian Salary, Minister of
Hillcrest Church of Christ
1939 snapfinger RD, Decatur, GA,
30035

# DON'T WORRY, BE HAPPY!

One of the things I enjoy the most is being outside and enjoying nature. What can I say? I'm from Florida. I enjoy the outdoors, the sun, and even the humidity. I wouldn't necessarily call myself a "bird watcher," but I enjoy watching birds. They fly with grace and so effortlessly. I don't know if you're like me or not, but one of the things I often wonder is how birds get enough food to survive. There are a lot of birds in the world; is there enough food for all of them?

I'm sure you know where this conversation is headed by now, right? In the King James Version of the gospel of Matthew chapter 6, verses 26-27, it says: Behold the fowls of the air: for they sow not, neither do they reap, nor gather into barns; yet your heavenly Father feedeth them. Are ye not much better than they? Which of you by taking thought can add one cubit unto his stature?

But listen to how it reads from the New Living Translation: Look at the birds. They don't plant or harvest or store food in barns, for your heavenly Father feeds them. And aren't you far more valuable to him than they are? Can all your worries add a single moment to your life? That's good news! These two verses indicate that we are more valuable and essential than birds. Yet, God still takes time to ensure the birds have what they need to survive. That being the case, why wouldn't God ensure we have everything we need to survive as well? God takes care of something as minor and insignificant as a bird, then we ought not worry about God not taking care of us.

Ultimately, these verses say to us: "Don't worry, be happy."
Let go of worries that God already has under control. When you worry less, you free up more time to embrace happiness in the present. Conversely, when you allow worries to consume you, you often find yourself less able to enjoy the present moment. Highlighting the futility of worrying can invoke a sense of relief and encourage the audience to focus on the present. While there may be several reasons that worrying is not good, allow me to give you two:

1. Worrying is tied to anxiety: Luke 12:26 says, "'Since you cannot do this very little thing, why do you worry about the rest?'"
2. Worrying is tied to a lack of faith in God: Luke 12:28 says, "If that is how God clothes the grass of the field, which is here today, and tomorrow is thrown into the fire, how much more will He clothe you—you of little faith!'"
So, let me encourage you to keep your joy and happiness. Don't allow them to fade by adding unnecessary worry and anxiety to the equation. Therefore, the "mic-drop" question becomes, 'Can worrying add any additional time to your life?' Can you worry and extend your life? Can you be bogged down with anxiety and live a long, healthy life? According to the Gospel of Matthew, the answer seems to be NO. As Bobby McFerrin wisely encouraged us to do way back in 1988, let's remember his simple yet profound message: Don't worry, be happy. This message, when applied to our lives, can reinforce our sense of reassurance and encourage us to trust in God's providence.

# Magnificent Men's Of God

# Magnificent Men's Of God

# Beauty Queen Over 60

# Veronica Etheridge

Veronica Etheridge was born and raised in the beautiful city of Charleston, South Carolina. Veronica has always considered her relationship with God and her family a priority. She attended Saint Augustine's University in Raleigh NC and also Liberty University of Lynchburg, Virginia, where she majored in Accounting and Entrepreneurship maintaining a 4.0 GPA. Veronica is a current member of the Beta Alpha Psi International Honor Organization. She is the mother of four beautiful adult children. Veronica worked in Corporate America for 15 years before she retired. When Veronica isn't traveling, she spends time with family and friends in Chicago, IL for 38 years and Los Angeles, CA for 3 years where she currently resides between both cities. She owns VTE Luxury Travel & Special Events which includes her travel business and special event planning. Veronica is also a first time author. Her book 'Intertwined', is Veronica's first book in which she expresses unconditional love for a person from her past, which will be released Fall 2024. She is currently writing her second book, 'The Freedom to Express Love', which is the sequel to her first. In her spare time, Ms. Etheridge enjoys reading, listening to jazz music, and traveling.

# Beauty Queen Over 60

## URENNA NFC CRAWFORD

### The Strong Female Lead

Inspirational Motivator

# Urenna' N.F.C Crawford

A Unique, Anointed Inspirational Motivator

The Author of **LEGACY: The Things Mommy Said to Me, I Say to You Again, and Say It, I was born to WIN!** Mrs. Crawford is a retired Educator who loves teaching. She attended Livingstone College as an Education major with a minor in Speech Communication. She has retired after thirty years of experience in Education.

She has had the opportunity to enrich the lives of students in the Rochester (NY) City School System (Teacher of the Year), Charlotte (NC), Mecklenburg School System (Teacher of the System), Wake County School System Raleigh (NC) and DeKalb County School System Decatur (GA) and the Head Start Program Supervisory Teacher. She was also recruited for Central Piedmont College Charlotte (NC) as a GED Teacher. She has

served students in Ghana, West Africa and Costa Rica. She has also worked as the Supervisor of Circulation for the Dana Cotton Library at Rutgers University in Newark, NJ and in the Bursar's office of Finance and Scholarships for eight years.

God has blessed her with His spirit and garnished her with grace and brightness. Her exuberance is with the gift of expression, creativity, motivation, seasoned with love and a sense of humor. You will find her honored in the Library of Congress's Who's Who as a "Southern Personality." She was honored by the Charlotte Post as a "Unique Black Woman."

She is a woman of God; who has a passion for teaching with God's gift of wisdom and oratorical skills; she has been able to inspire the young and mature throughout her life and remain creative, passionate and strong as she persevered. Mrs. Crawford's tenet is that everyone has something unique to offer.

She began a second career of fifteen years with IBM Corporation, where she retired as a Customer Service Manager. She was certified in Business Administration from Sigma Business College of IBM. While working full time, she completed a certification in Early Childhood Education at Spelman College.

Mrs. Crawford mentored The Miss Georgia Black Teen Pageant, resulting in the contestant winning First Place. She developed monologues for students to audition for Oratorical Contest to enter the Schools of Fine Arts, all were accepted. She served as the Drama Director for the General Baptist Association, Drama Director and Founder for the Utopians' Drama Ensemble. One of her protégés recently received an Oscar for her performance on Broadway.

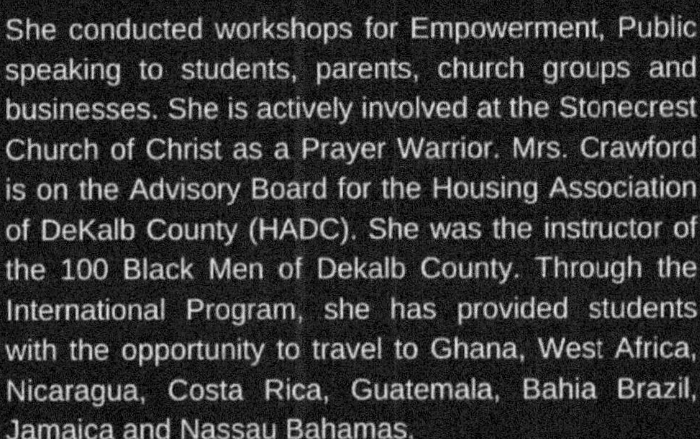

She conducted workshops for Empowerment, Public speaking to students, parents, church groups and businesses. She is actively involved at the Stonecrest Church of Christ as a Prayer Warrior. Mrs. Crawford is on the Advisory Board for the Housing Association of DeKalb County (HADC). She was the instructor of the 100 Black Men of Dekalb County. Through the International Program, she has provided students with the opportunity to travel to Ghana, West Africa, Nicaragua, Costa Rica, Guatemala, Bahia Brazil, Jamaica and Nassau Bahamas.

Mrs. Crawford is confident that beauty flows from the heart, illuminating one's character and moral qualities. Her confidence has been developed through life's experiences and personal development.

She knows her wellness comes from God. Eating foods that are good for her and staying physically active are a must as one matures. She keeps a positive attitude while interacting with individuals who enrich her life. Her health care is now paramount. Mrs. Crawford has learned to leverage her unique qualities, realizing there is no one else in the world like her.

**"Wearing my red lipstick, it makes me feel incredible!"**

She has learned to make herself a priority,

**"asking God for guidance."**

Mrs. Crawford knows that external beauty will fade. Having confidence that she is capable of coping with her emotions, gives her value and clarity. She says,

**"Knowing my purpose in life is personally meaningful and of consequences to the world beyond myself. I Was Born to Win."**

# Earnestine Grant

Born April 1951 in Mississippi, as a baby she was relocated to Alabama. Graduated from Green County High School in a little town called Boligee Ala. Following her childhood dream to become a Nurse she moved to Tuscaloosa Ala. Only to find out that she would have to work as a candy stripper at the local hospital. Being out on your own you need to get paid if you are working. So, she went to a junior college and took her second love which is sewing. She later meets and marries what became her daughters' father. The marriage ended and Earnestine moved to Los Angeles Ca. Where she immediately enrolled in nursing school. She worked days and went to school at night. Determined now even more so as a mother of two little girls to begin her lifelong dream of becoming a Nurse, the proudest day of her life was when she graduated from nursing school with a job already lined up. She worked as a Nurse for forty years and still uses her nursing skills daily caring for her youngest daughter who was injured in a hit and run auto accident that left her paralyzed October 23, 2004. She later remarried and had two more daughters five years after the marriage ended. Now four daughters and a single mother, as a strong believer in God she stood on His word, prayed and waited for twenty-five years single God answered her prayers at sixty-one. They were introduced to by a mutual family member that knew both situations, he was two years widowed and she was single so the grandmother of her grandchild and youngest daughter made a love connection "he that finds a wife finds a good thing". They celebrated their tenth-year anniversary last September. Seventy-three retired from nursing and she has a custom sewing and alteration business, and she is launching her custom T-Shirt business. Four daughters, sixteen grandchildren and twelve great grandchildren and one on the way. By His Grace life is good. It may not have always been easy but God... living my life

## HAROLENE COOK

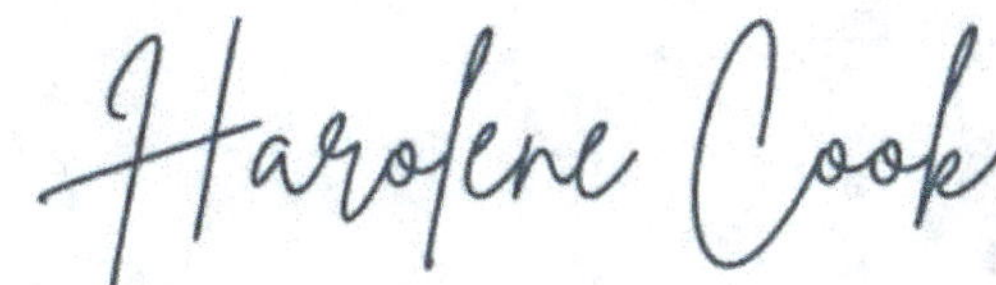

# Harolene Cook

## Lover of Life and People

Harolene was born in Miami, Florida, in 1955 to Mr. Harold and Doris Williams. From an early age, she discovered her passions for baking, fashion, interior design, and serving others.

Harolene's love for baking was inspired by her mother's renowned homemade dishes and the way meals facilitated family time. To nurture her passion for interior design, she would meticulously rearrange the family's furniture, transforming the ambiance without incurring costs.

Her commitment to serving others was solidified when she became a teenage bride and mother. These significant life events not only altered her path to college but also defined her life's purpose. The foundation of family first, instilled by her parents, guided how she raised her three children and operated as a spouse. As the family matriarch, her mission is to impart biblical teachings and to plant seeds of kindness, community, and love in her grandchildren and extended family.

In addition to her family responsibilities, Harolene's compassion for service led her into a 47-year career. She worked as a Savings Counselor at Chase Federal Savings and Loans for ten years, a Secretary at the State Attorney's Office for ten years, and a Certified Fire Rescue Dispatcher and Certified Trainer for twenty-seven years, before retiring in 2017.

Retirement has not slowed her pace; she volunteered at Piedmont Medical and is currently a dedicated member of The Stonecrest Church of Christ, under the teachings of Dr. Richard L. Barclay. She is also a member of The Red Hat Society and The Black Diva Association, fully embracing her talents in interior design. Her latest interior design project was featured in a magazine, highlighting her attention to detail and ability to create a visual masterpiece.

# Sharon Britton

I am a 71 year old, retired mother of 3. 2 sons Adrian and Aaron and a daughter Angela. I have 3 wonderful grandchildren, 2 boys and a girl; who are my whole world. I adore my grandchildren and cherish every moment with them. I absolutely love God and family.

For 35 years, I worked for Northwestern Mutual Insurance company, retiring in April of 2008. I've been blessed to enjoy retirement. I am married to Norman Britton, and we will be celebrating 22 years together in June of this year. What's cool about that, is that we are still honeymooning!

I am a proud Seasoned Saint. I'm enjoying the life that God has given me. My greatest achievement has been to raise my children. My passion is caring, especially for my family. My hobbies are traveling, reading, and listening to music. However, my "new-found" hobby is non-professional/amateur acting. The challenge and fun of this activity is creating your character. I'm so grateful and blessed to have made 3 scores and 10.

God made me, loves me and cares about me. Old age is God's reward for godliness. I give God all honor, praise and glory.

Norman Britton, her husband is her everything.

# Phyllis Flynn

Phyllis Flynn is a seasoned professional with a passion for technology, business, and education. With a bachelor's degree in business, Phyllis embarked on her career in the technology field in 1986, marking the beginning of a remarkable journey. For over three decades, Phyllis dedicated her expertise to the federal government in the technology department.

Starting as a Computer Programmer, Phyllis quickly demonstrated her exceptional skills and work ethic, leading to various promotions throughout her tenure.

Throughout her career, Phyllis received numerous awards for her outstanding service and excellence in training. Her passion for technology and education converged, leading her to excel in introductory technology training. This role brought her great joy as she imparted her knowledge to others and witnessed their growth and development. Following a fulfilling career in government service, Phyllis transitioned into entrepreneurship, founding a successful construction company in 2014, which remains operational to this day.

In 2022, she embarked on her most recent entrepreneurial endeavor, driven by her enduring passion for education and technology. Returning to the digital sector, Phyllis established a new business venture—teaching individuals how to develop and deliver their own online courses through:

https://www.learntocreatecourses.com/

Drawing from her years of experience and expertise, she guides aspiring educators through the process of crafting engaging and impactful online courses, with a lens on including women in underserved communities. Beyond her professional pursuits, Phyllis is an avid reader and gardener. With a thirst for knowledge, she immerses herself in a wide range of literature, constantly expanding her horizons and staying abreast of the latest industry trends. In her garden, she finds solace and fulfillment, nurturing vibrant plants and creating a serene oasis.

Phyllis Flynn is a remarkable individual whose career and passions intertwine in a harmonious blend of technology, business, and education. Her relentless pursuit of excellence, combined with her love for learning and teaching, continues to shape her journey and inspire those around her.

# BIOGRAPHY

### AUDREY BEHARIE-McGEE

FINE ARTIST/
PHOTOGRAPHER

audreybehariemcgee@gmail.com

**AudreyBeharieMcGee.com**

British born Audrey Beharie-McGee is a self-taught emerging fine artist and photographer who now resides in Atlanta, GA., USA & London, UK and is married to storyboard artist and fine artist, Brian McGee.

Audrey is also a singer/songwriter and performing arts coach and has always had an enormous vibrant energy, especially for singing and performing, which has fueled her creative and artistic pizzazz. From an early age, she was constantly curious about the world around her and challenged herself to explore a myriad of interesting, entrepreneurial and exhilarating adventures.

In 1988, whilst working for avid art collectors, **Sir Paul McCartney and the late Linda McCartney** at their offices in London, UK, Audrey developed an appreciation for the fine arts, where she was able to come face-to-face with some of the world's most prolific abstract, pop and impressionists artists of our time. She became intimately familiar with the neo-impressionism of **Vincent Van Gogh** and was particularly touched by the psychedelic canvas works of **Peter Max,** and entralled by the pop, collage and abstract artwork of **Andy Warhol, Robert Rauschenberg** and **Jackson Pollock.** Audrey's eyes, soul and spirit was able to experience the full impact and energy of these incredible artists, their works and the intricate interweaving of paint, colors, fabrication, media and elements that brought these canvases to life!

Unfortunately, in 2015 Audrey was diagnosed with Hashimotos - an auto-immune condition which, sadly, resulted in a host of debilitating health conditions including the deterioration of her vocal chords, hampering her ability to sing. This was a devastating blow to Audrey especially affecting her creative spirit. However, whilst on a cruise, Audrey and Brian were invited to attend an art gallery event and immediately, she felt that long-lost fire in her spirit rekindled as she re-discovered her love, excitement and appreciation for art! GOD had opened up another door for her which is full of endless possibilities!

On her return to Georgia, Audrey wasted no time in immersing herself into her new love and began with earnest, to study and embrace the works of her favorite artist. And, on her journey, she was then to discover the incredible talents of many black artists such as **Rashid Johnson, Howardena Pindell, Mark Bradford, David Driskell, Janet Henry, Kehinde Wiley, Charles Alston, Jacob Lawrence** and of course, the late great **Jean Michel Basquiat** which have fueled the flame and became increasingly fascinated by the way in which these artists would create their works with such uninhibited freedom.

With intense hues, varied tones and organic materials, Audrey feels that every scrape of a pallet knife, splat of splashed paint, tear of paper and dab of acrylic or watercolor allows her imagination to soar and run free. And, with integrating her photography work with her mixed media art, Audrey is driven by her passion to explore new forms of expression.

Through the creation of visual art, Audrey has found familiar territory to that of composing a well-crafted song which, expresses all the integral facets of superb lyrics, well-crafted instrumentation, subtle melody, sultry harmonies and cadence, work in concert to create BEAUTY!

Audrey has shown her work in London, UK, Atlanta, USA, Venice and Rome, Italy and was also had a residency at the celebrated Rossocinabro Gallery in Rome, Italy.

# Audrey Is a Winner

# Annette Goudeau

My name is Annette Goudeau and I am 67 years old. I finished high school at Rezin Orr High School and did two years of college at Malcolm X College. I've always been in the field of

helping people. First, as a CNA in the Chicago land area for 25 years.

In 2004 I built a 5000 square foot house, and in 2014 I turned that house into a homeless shelter for abused and battered women. The shelter is called Evergreen Safe House. Darnial Miller and I have run the shelter for several years. By the grace of God, we are still in existence. We are always open to donations for housing the women. We are also open to grant writers who would like to donate their time in writing a grant for the shelter. May God bless you all in your endeavors.

Gofundme Link: <u>Fundraiser by Annette Goudeau : Evergreen safehouse for abused and battered women. (gofundme.com)</u>

# Delores A. Martin

I am a devout Christian, going to the Stonecrest Church of Christ in McDonough, Georgia. I currently reside in Jefferson, Georgia.

My name is Dolores A. Martin, I was born in South Carolina in 1955. When I was two, my parents moved to Michigan. I graduated from Mount Clemens High in Michigan, after which I started working for Chrysler Corporation. I stayed there for 31 years until my retirement.

I got married at 19 and subsequently had 4 children. At the age of 45, my first husband passed away, after which I was left to raise three children by myself with an eleven-month-old baby. I stayed single for 22 years until I met this wonderful man named Robert Martin, who I am currently married to.

All that I am, and all that I have, I credit to my Lord and Savior Jesus Christ. I thank Him for His love, grace, and mercy. Whatever you do in life, put God above all else and He will direct your steps on the right path.

*"Life has not always been easy in my 68 years on this Earth, but God can take you through whatever you are going through, if you put your trust in Him."*

# Angelous Sparks – Young Bey

Angelous Sparks-Young Bey was born in Macon, Ga. She is currently 67 years old. She attended Mercer University, Macon, Ga. BA in Mental Retardation/ Special Education Graduate studies. Some of her work experiences include serving as:

- Administration, Ga State University
- Certified Teacher Specialist
- Certified Related Vocational Instruction Specialist
- Chair/Lead Instructor for entering students with Special Needs to Alpha Alternative School
- Chairperson for IEP Meetings, Alpha Alternative School
- Rockdale City Alpha Alternative School
- Workshop Facilitator
- Coordinator of Service Learning Program, Alpha Alternative School
- Administrative Assistant, Alpha Alternative School
- Retired, Rockdale County Schools

Objective: To Teach, direct, guide, and support students who are at-risk and have special needs

Passion: To Serve God and the community through the homeless and Litter Ministry.

"*God allows me to be a light to those in the dark…*"

Poetic
Panorama

# Never Apologize

Never Apologize My Black People for who you are,
Never apologize for your weeping and tired eyes
which can be seen from afar.
Never apologize for your black royalty of the Kings
and Queens from who you are,
Never apologize for your black ancestors who
struggled long and hard.
Never apologize for your beautiful black skin,
For Being both Black AND Beautiful,
was Always a win,
Never was it meant to be your end.
Never apologize for celebrating and honoring
the contributions, culture and resilience long
unrecognized.
Never apologize for the achievements of black
individuals' through-out the history of this land,
For all have contributed whether it be a woman or
a man.
Never apologize.
I say to you NEVER EVER Apologize
for celebrating the richness of our legacy.
You see, Many black leaders fought for justice,
some of them dying so that you and I could be free.
Changing lives so that WE can be the best that we
can be.
Never apologize!
Stand tall black people,
Face Your challenges of today.
You were born to win, what else I can say!
Never Having to apologize means WAKE UP!
It's time to stop sleeping as life passes by!
Make a total commitment educate oneself,
and you won't ask why..
Let's Not repeat the history of failures
because we chose to sleep instead of waking up.
Once awakened, we No longer remain in darkness..

instead we have become a shining light.
That which was wrong must now be made right!
Never apologize for someone who does not
understand you or how you feel.
Just remember, There are gifts and talents in
each one of you.
You are leaders and future leaders
Take Your Stand.
Build for future generations so they can stand.
So... Never Apologize
Now that you understand, only apologize..
If You Refuse To Give or lend a hand.

by:

Dr. Alice
Teague

# Isolated Breathing

I feel like I'm boxed in,
I'm trapped under expectations I can't meet,
so much I can barely breathe.
All the doubts and mistakes packed in.
Circumstances where they say "stress is normal,"
those same people are the ones to crumble
when the stress becomes too much,
because that's the thing, stress isn't normal.
People shouldn't have to crumble
when every suppressed emotion they have erupts,
and they feel like they can't breathe
but they can't breathe.
It's not just other's expectations, it's theirs,
people suffocate themselves in distraction
so they can't see their mistakes,
but they shouldn't do it to the point
they deceive themselves and they can't heal.
They can't breathe,
24/7 anxiety and nobody is able to breathe.
The world's expectations dropped on everybody's shoulders
and they can't breathe.
But it's not like they didn't create these expectations themselves,
Society is based on self sabotage and now it's crumbling,
and we can't breathe.
But if only it were from the lack of oxygen,
then maybe there would be one person
who was still able to breathe.
That one person, breathing while others are suffocating.
That one person, persevering despite other's suffering.
That one person, thinking they're weak because
they haven't gone through what others have.
That one person, who everyone thinks is strong
because they haven't gone through what they have.
Some are trying to help, trying to push them forward.
Others, jealous of their strength.
They try to pull them down with them.

They lie, they deceive, they spit on them and say it's raining.
They cover the sun and say it's cloudy.
They curtain the hope and spotlight the despair of reality.
That one person, ripping apart all hopeful thoughts,
This is the reason hate spreads .
That one person, whose thoughts are now corrupted by the
thoughts of others.
But then they find that one person who gets rid of the negative
thoughts
and replaces them with hopeful ones.
That one person, who helps them see the sun through the clouds.
That one person, who is the glasses to their eyes.
That one person, who helps them see the deception
through the words that were branded as love.
That one person, who helps them see others' deception is not
love,
and that our mistakes don't define us.
That one person who makes us believe in ourselves
and makes other's thoughts towards us dissipate in our minds,
They make us free of the influence of others.
The ridicule and hurt from others that have deceived me,
are now just shadows in the back of my mind.
I have finally cleaned my slate.
The freedom of society's expectations is what gave me the
courage to dance.
Now I can breathe.

Oratorical Showcase

by Devin Swims
age 13 &
Serenity
Chandler age 14

# O. J. Simpson, The Legacy

The name O.J. Simpson conjures a spectrum of memories and emotions for many, reflecting a life marked by extraordinary athletic achievement and profound personal controversies. Born Orenthal James Simpson on July 8, 1947, he emerged from the challenging neighborhoods of San Francisco to become one of the most celebrated running backs in the history of American football. His story is one of triumph, turmoil, and the complex human experience.

## Athletic Prowess and Football Glory

Simpson's journey to football greatness began at the University of Southern California (USC), where he dazzled fans and critics alike with his speed, agility, and determination. His standout performances earned him the coveted Heisman Trophy in 1968, an accolade that solidified his status as a collegiate football legend. This success paved the way for a remarkable professional career.

In the NFL, Simpson's name became synonymous with excellence. Playing primarily for the Buffalo Bills over 11 seasons, he set numerous records and became the first player to rush for more than 2,000 yards in a single season, achieving this milestone in 1973. His contributions to the game were not just in his statistics but in the way he played, bringing excitement and a new level of athleticism to the sport. Simpson's number 32 jersey became iconic, and his on-field prowess earned him a place in the Pro Football Hall of Fame in 1985.

## Beyond the Field: A Cultural Icon

Simpson's charisma and charm extended beyond the football field. He became a prominent figure in popular culture, transitioning into acting and broadcasting. His roles in movies like "The Towering Inferno" and the "Naked Gun" series showcased his versatility and endeared him to a broader audience. As a sports commentator, he brought insight and enthusiasm to the game he loved, further cementing his legacy as a multifaceted talent.

## Reflecting on a Legacy

As we reflect on O.J. Simpson's life, it's essential to acknowledge the full tapestry of his experiences—both the remarkable achievements and the profound challenges. His story reminds us that human lives are rarely simple; they are woven with triumphs and trials, moments of glory, and times of profound struggle.

Simpson's contribution to the game of football is undeniable. His legacy on the field continues to inspire new generations of athletes who admire his skill, determination, and the barriers he broke in his athletic career. Despite the controversies that clouded his later years, the impact he had on sports and popular culture remains significant.

Many of us can remember the late O.J. Simpson; one of the greatest running backs in our Black History, playing 11 seasons with the Buffalo Bills. He recently died from prostate cancer, at age 74.

Despite the turbulence and turmoil that marked the later years of his life, Simpson's contribution to the game of football was undeniable. As we reflect on his highly publicized life, it is essential to be mindful of the complexities of the human experience. While Simpson's actions may have sparked controversy and debate, it's important to offer our compassion, respect, and understanding to his family and friends.

In the end, O.J. Simpson's journey reminds us that life is a tapestry

woven with both triumphs and trials. Even though O.J. Simpson is no longer with us, we cannot forget that he left an indelible mark on the world of sports. Let us also heed the timeless wisdom in the saying:

"Let he who is without sin, cast the first stone".

May Simpson find peace in the next chapter of his journey and may his legacy on the football field continue to inspire generations to come.

*From the host of The Dr. Alice Show, Atlanta TV 1061, and the author of Spotlight Spectacular magazine .*

*Rest in peace*
*Orenthal James (O.J.) Simpson*

*July 8, 1947 to April 10, 2024*

# O. J. SIMPSON

## A Legacy of Triumph and Turmoil

O.J. Simpson passed away on April 10, 2024, from prostate cancer. As we bid farewell, it is crucial to extend compassion and understanding to his family and friends. His journey through life, with all its complexities, serves as a poignant reminder of our shared humanity.

May O.J. Simpson find peace in his next chapter, and may his legacy on the football field continue to inspire and motivate.

Rest in peace, Orenthal James Simpson. Your mark on the world of sports will never be forgotten.

RESTAURANT ENTREPRENEUR AND AUTHOR

# FANNIE MAE HOUSER

SHARES HER RECIPES

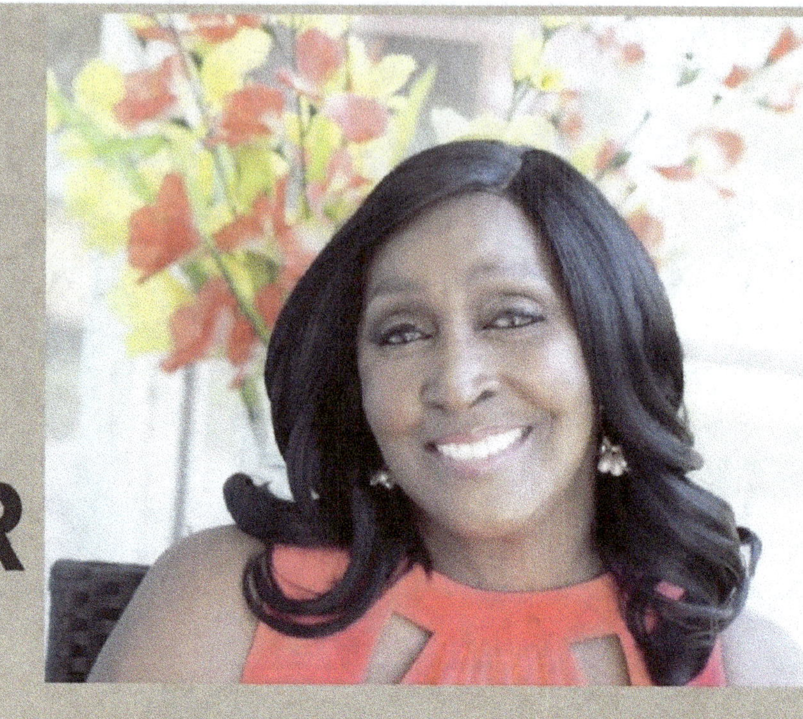

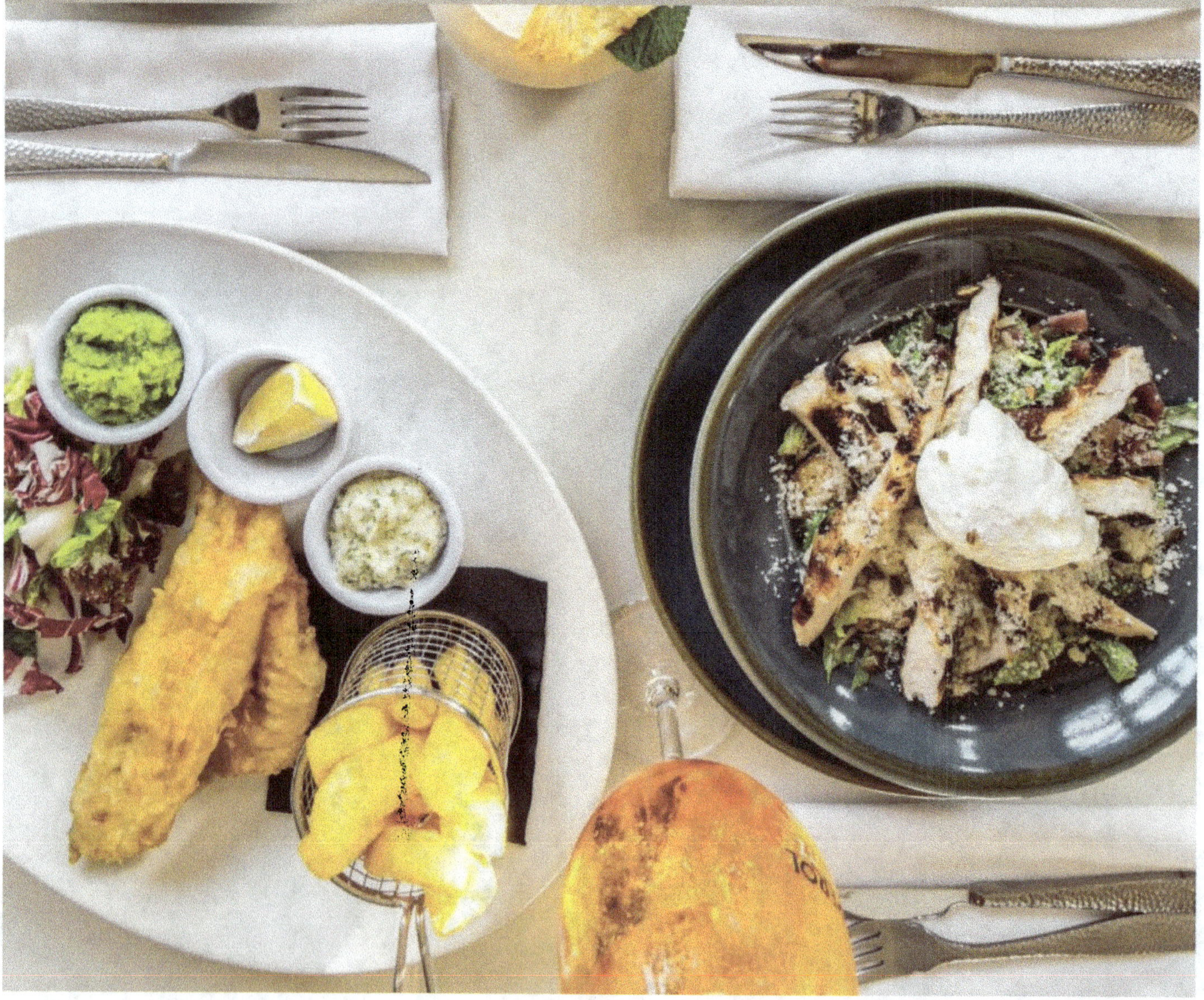

### Ingredients:

- 2 lbs chicken wings, separated into flats and drumettes
- 2 tablespoons olive oil
- 2 tablespoons unsalted butter, melted Zest of 1 lemon
- 2 tablespoons lemon juice
- 1 teaspoon lemon pepper seasoning
- 1/2 teaspoon garlic powder
- 1/2 teaspoon onion powder
- Salt and pepper to taste
- Chopped fresh parsley for garnish (optional) Lemon wedges for serving

### Instructions:

Preheat your air fryer to 400°F (200°C) for about 5 minutes.

In a large mixing bowl, combine olive oil, melted unsalted butter, lemon zest, lemon juice, lemon pepper seasoning, garlic powder, onion powder, salt, and pepper. Mix until well combined.

Add the chicken wings to the bowl and toss until they are evenly coated with the lemon butter mixture. Place the seasoned chicken wings in the preheated air fryer basket in a single layer, making sure they are not overcrowded.

Air fry the chicken wings at 400°F (200°C) for 25-30 minutes, flipping halfway through the cooking time, or until they are golden brown and crispy.

Once cooked, remove the chicken wings from the air fryer basket and transfer them to a serving plate. Garnish with chopped fresh parsley, if desired, and serve hot with lemon wedges on the side for squeezing over the wings.

**Enjoy the tangy and flavorful Air Fryer Buttery Lemon Pepper Chicken Wings as a delicious appetizer or snack!**

## BAKED LEMON CHICKEN

**Ingredients:**

- 3 Tbsp lemon juice
- 1 tsp fresh lemon zest
- 1 Tbsp finely chopped onion
- ¼ tsp paprika
- 2 Tbsp olive oil
- Dash of salt
- Fresh-ground pepper
- 2 whole, boneless, skinless chicken breasts, halved

1. Preheat the oven to 400 degrees. In a small bowl, combine all ingredients except chicken.
2. Place chicken in a shallow baking dish and pour the lemon mixture over it. Bake for 45 minutes until the chicken is no longer pink.
3. Transfer chicken to a serving platter, spoon juices over it, and serve.

**4 Servings**
**Serving Size 3 oz**

AMOUNT PER SERVING

**Exchanges**
3 Lean Meat
1/ 2 Fat

**Calories** 205
**Calories from Fat** 88
**Total Fat** 10 g
**Saturated Fat** 2 g
**Cholesterol** 72 mg
**Sodium** 100 mg
**Total Carbohydrate** 1 g
**Dietary Fiber** 0 g
**Sugars** 0 g
**Protein** 27 g

## GRILLED CHICKEN WITH GARLIC

**Ingredients**

- 4 3-oz boneless, skinless chicken
- breast halves
- 2 Tbsp canola oil (divided use)
- 1 cup red wine
- 3 sprigs thyme
- 5 garlic cloves, minced
- 5 garlic cloves, whole and unpeeled
- Fresh ground pepper

1. In a plastic zippered bag, place chicken, 1 Tbsp oil, wine, thyme, and minced garlic. Marinate for 2 to 3 hours in the refrigerator.

2. Preheat the oven to 375 degrees.

3. Spread whole garlic cloves on a cookie sheet, drizzle with remaining oil, and sprinkle it with pepper. Bake for 30 minutes, stirring occasionally, until soft.

4. When cool, squeeze garlic paste from cloves and mash in a small bowl with a fork .

5. Remove chicken from marinade and grill for 12 to 15 minutes, turning frequently and brushing with garlic paste. Transfer to a platter and serve hot.

**4 Servings**
**Serving Size 3 oz**

AMOUNT PER SERVING

**Exchanges**
4 Lean Meat

**Calories** 217
**Calories from Fat** 91
**Total Fat** 10 g
**Saturated Fat** 1 g
**Cholesterol** 73 mg
**Sodium** 65 mg
**Total Carbohydrate** 2 g
**Dietary Fiber** 0 g
**Sugars** 0 g
**Protein** 27 g

## APPLE CINNAMON PORK CHOPS

**Ingredients:**
- 2 tsp canola oil
- 1 large apple, sliced
- ¼ tsp cinnamon
- ⅛ tsp nutmeg
- 2 3-oz lean boneless pork chops, trimmed of fat

1. In a medium nonstick skillet, heat the canola oil. Add apple slices and saute until just tender. Sprinkle with cinnamon and nutmeg, remove from heat, and keep warm.

2. Place pork chops in a skillet and cook thoroughly. Remove pork chops from skillet, arrange on a serving platter, spoon apple slices on top, and serve.

**2 Servings**
**Serving Size 1 pork chop with apples**

AMOUNT PER SERVING

**Exchanges**
1 Fruit
2 Lean Meat
1 Fat
**Calories** 212
**Calories from Fat** 92
**Total Fat** 10 g
**Saturated Fat** 2 g
**Cholesterol** 44 mg
**Sodium** 36 mg
**Total Carbohydrate** 15 g
**Dietary Fiber** 3 g
**Sugars** 11 g
**Protein** 16 g

## BAKED LEMON CHICKEN

**Ingredients:**

- 3 Tbsp lemon juice
- 1 tsp fresh lemon zest
- 1 Tbsp finely chopped onion
- ¼ tsp paprika
- 2 Tbsp olive oil
- Dash of salt
- Fresh-ground pepper
- 2 whole, boneless, skinless chicken breasts, halved

1. Preheat the oven to 400 degrees. In a small bowl, combine all ingredients except chicken.
2. Place chicken in a shallow baking dish and pour the lemon mixture over it. Bake for 45 minutes until the chicken is no longer pink.
3. Transfer chicken to a serving platter, spoon juices over it, and serve.

**4 Servings**
**Serving Size 3 oz**

AMOUNT PER SERVING

**Exchanges**
3 Lean Meat
1/ 2 Fat

**Calories** 205
**Calories from Fat** 88
**Total Fat** 10 g
**Saturated Fat** 2 g
**Cholesterol** 72 mg
**Sodium** 100 mg
**Total Carbohydrate** 1 g
**Dietary Fiber** 0 g
**Sugars** 0 g
**Protein** 27 g

## GRILLED CHICKEN WITH GARLIC

**Ingredients**

- 4 3-oz boneless, skinless chicken
- breast halves
- 2 Tbsp canola oil (divided use)
- 1 cup red wine
- 3 sprigs thyme
- 5 garlic cloves, minced
- 5 garlic cloves, whole and unpeeled
- Fresh ground pepper

# BLACKBERRY & BLUEBERRY OAT CRUMBLES

**Ingredients:**

**Fruits:**
- ⅔ cups granulated sugar
- 1 Tbsp cornstarch
- 2 pints blueberries (about 4.5 cups)
- 1 pint blackberries
- 1 Tbsp fresh lemon juice

**Topping:**
- 1 cup all purpose flour
- ¾ cup old-fashioned oats
- ½ cup packed brown sugar
- ½ cup (1 stick cold) butter cut into pieces
- ½ tsp ground cinnamon
- 3 Tbsp finely chopped crystallized ginger

**Fruit:** Preheat oven to 375°F. In a bowl, mix granulated sugar and cornstarch. Add blueberries, blackberries, and lemon juice, toss to coat. Divide berry mixture evenly among 8 (6 oz) ramekins

**Topping:** In the same bowl, combine flour, oats and brown sugar. With fingertips, work in butter and cinnamon until coarse crumbs form; mix in crystallized ginger. Crumble topping over fruit. Place ramekins on a large rimmed baking sheet. Bake for 30 minutes, or until topping browns and fruit is bubbly. Cool on a wire rack and serve warm or at room temperature.

Makes 8 servings.

# PINEAPPLE UPSIDE DOWN MIMOSAS

Elevate your brunch with this delightful twist on the classic mimosa. The Pineapple Upside Down Mimosa combines the tropical sweetness of pineapple juice with the unique flavor of cake-flavored vodka, all topped off with crisp Brut champagne. Garnished with a pineapple wedge and a maraschino cherry, this cocktail is not only delicious but also visually stunning. Perfect for celebrations or a refreshing start to your weekend.

## Ingredients:

- 1/2 cup Brut champagne, chilled
- 1/2 cup pineapple juice, chilled
- 1 ounce cake-flavored vodka
- 1 pineapple wedge
- Maraschino cherry

## Directions:

1. In a champagne flute, combine pineapple juice, vodka, and champagne.
2. Garnish with a pineapple wedge and maraschino cherry.

**Prep Time:** 5 minutes
**Total Time:** 5 minutes
**Servings:** 1

# ROSHAUNDA YANCY

BOLD AND
BRIGHT

SINGLE
MOTHER

# ROSHAUNDA YANCY

Roshaunda Yancy is a single mother with two children who defies expectations and overcomes obstacles to achieve outstanding success. Despite the challenges in raising her children alone and juggling the demands of a full-time job; Roshaunda Yancy made a bold decision to return to school to pursue her academic dreams. Her unwavering commitment to her studies paid off as she achieved a stellar 4.0 GPA, showing her exceptional intelligence and drive.

Roshaunda Yancy faced numerous challenges from late nights of studying to balancing her personal and professional life. Despite these hurdles, she remained focused and emerged victorious. This heartwarming story of her life celebrates the incredible journey and highlights her as a beacon of inspiration to other women, who are also striving to achieve their goals against all odds.

Through Roshaunda Yancy's story we have witnessed the transformative power of resilience and the importance of never giving up on one's dreams.

Congratulation Ms. Yancy for being a beacon of hope in the world we live in.

# STAY HEALTHY AT ANY AGE
## WITH WYNITA WALTHER

## Unlock The Secret to Ageless Living

You Youthful and Energized at Any Age

Discover How Emotional, Spiritual, and Mental Wellness Can Keep

The Best Looks of the Season

My name is Wynita and I am starting a movement. Almost 5 years ago, I started my coaching business, combining faith, fitness, therapeutic practices & personal development designed for ambitious women. In today's fast-paced world, the pursuit of health and wellness is more indispensable that ever, and has also become a very multi-faceted journey.

My transformation began in my 30s after a 20-year heartbreaking relationship ended, and I found myself exhausted from living in the rat race. Through this hard work, I built a dream career getting paid to travel the world and experience the most incredible luxuries available, working in the hedge fund and finance industries. But after 15 years of working in finance, I realized that my emotional and mental health had taken a backseat. It was then that I decided to prioritize my overall well-being. I discovered that true fitness is not just about physical health but also about nurturing the mind, heart, and soul. As fate would have it, as I was getting healthy, stronger and, living my best life, most people were aggressively gaining weight and battling the effects of depression & the COVID-19 pandemic. So, in 2020 I started my coaching business, combining faith, fitness, therapeutic practices & personal development. In 2021, I pursued my next level of peace and left the finance industry, moved from my big city lifestyle to an incredible small town in Texas; where I met my husband & which also inspired growing the Faith Queens community.

Maybe similar to some of you- even though I had a loving & faith-filled family, I grew up with some
anxiety and lacked key skills to make my dreams a reality. Hungry for the knowledge to live my life to
the fullest, I was led to train under international leaders, godly multimillionaire entrepreneurs & strategists, whose focus was primarily about philanthropy for over 15 years. I've worked relentlessly on relationship skill development, therapy and a committed relationship with God. For almost 20 years, I've made choices and commitments to cultivate a faith that now gives me an incredible, purpose driven life.

I've started wynita.com with Faith Queens & Beauty for Ashes | Faith Queens Mentorship
because through the many mistakes & lots of heart break, I've found peace and love; through a deep understanding from studying Scripture, investing in my spiritual transformation and learning from some
of the best theology teachers and biblical thought leaders in the world.

**TIP: ESTABLISH A REGULAR SLEEP ROUTINE BY GOING TO BED AND WAKING UP AT THE SAME TIME EACH DAY.**

# STAY FRESH

I've surrounded myself in a community of women, leaders and entrepreneurs who apply the Word of God to every part of their life, and I see it work. Now, I help others do the same.

Beyond physical fitness and a balanced diet, true wellness includes community as well as emotional, spiritual, and mental health. As we age, maintaining long term life expectancy and quality of life with high energy is not just about exercise and eating right—it's also about nurturing the mind with faith, the heart with generosity, and the soul with love. Here are my eight secrets that can help anyone stay young and vibrant at any age.

1. - Stay Active - Find an activity that enriches your life and can also build healthy relationships.

Live mindfully and become aware of what your body needs. Daily walking outside if great for our health. Perhaps you can try pickleball or biking through your neighborhood. Find and practice a cardiovascular activity and if it uses a mind body connection during the exercise, like tennis or pickleball, even better. An active lifestyle and can-do attitude is a powerful tool for staying youthful.

Tip: Our thoughts and attitudes significantly impact our overall well-being. Engaging in activities that bring joy like healthy activity and exercise, spending time with loved ones, or simply enjoying nature, can boost your mood and energy levels.

2. Nurture Your Spiritual Health & Cultivate a Positive Mindset Spiritual wellness is often overlooked but is essential for overall health. Connecting with God can provide a sense of fresh energy, purpose and inner peace. Whether through prayer, meditation, or mindfulness practices, taking time to nurture your spiritual side can lead to profound emotional and mental benefits.
Tip: Practicing gratitude, focusing on the good in life, and maintaining an optimistic outlook can reduce stress and increase happiness. Dedicate a few minutes each day to spiritual practices. Whether it's meditation, prayer, or reading the Bible, this time can help you connect with your inner self and find tranquility in the chaos of daily life.

3. Stay Socially Connected - Feeling connected to a community Human beings are inherently social creatures. Maintaining strong relationships and a supportive social network is crucial for emotional and mental well-being. Loneliness and isolation can lead to depression and anxiety, while meaningful connections with family and friends can enhance your sense of belonging and happiness.
Tip: Make it a priority to stay connected with loved ones. Schedule regular catch-ups, join a church or groups that interest you, and be open to meeting new people. Social interactions can invigorate your spirit and keep you feeling young.

4. Be Inquisitive & Engage in Lifelong Learning
Keeping your mind active and engaged is vital for mental wellness. Engage in materials that light you up, and take action in areas that stretch your capacity. Intentionally challenging yourself to live according to what you see in your heart daily not only helps in keeping the brain sharp but also boosts self-confidence and keeps you motivated. Whether it's picking up a new hobby, getting a coach or mentor, reading a book, listening to a podcast or attending workshops, continuous learning can keep your mind agile and vibrant.

Tip: Read 10 pages a day and the book should be teaching you something. The excitement of new knowledge can reignite your passion for life and keep you mentally young.

5. Practice Emotional Resilience Emotional resilience is the ability to bounce back from life's challenges with grace and strength. Building emotional resilience involves acknowledging your feelings, managing stress effectively, and maintaining a balanced emotional state. Practices such as deep breathing, journaling, and seeking support from a therapist or counselor can enhance your emotional resilience.
Tip: Develop a personal toolkit for managing stress. This could include breathe work or relaxation techniques, regular physical activity, creative outlets like art or music, and talking to someone you trust.
Strengthening your emotional resilience will help you release unforgiveness and strengthens us to navigate life's ups and downs with greater ease and maintain your youthful energy.

6. Go Organic
Choosing organic foods can have a significant impact on your overall health. Organic produce is free from harmful pesticides and chemicals, ensuring that your body receives pure, nutrient-dense nourishment. This choice not only benefits your physical health but also supports mental and emotional well-being by reducing your exposure to toxins.

Tip: Incorporate more organic fruits and vegetables into your diet. Start with the dirty dozen, meats and dairy and options for the produce you consume most frequently. Then, gradually expand your choices.

7. Adopt a Healthy diet. A healthy diet is a cornerstone of well-being. Consuming low sugar, staying hydrated with plenty of water, and eating a variety of vegetables can boost your energy levels and keep your body functioning optimally. A balanced diet helps maintain a healthy weight, supports brain function, and enhances your mood.

Tip: Make your own as often as possible and plan your meals to include a variety of colorful vegetables. Limit sugary snacks and beverages, and drink at least eight glasses of water a day. This approach ensures you receive a wide range of nutrients necessary for overall health.

8. Prioritize sleep

Quality sleep is essential for maintaining high energy and a youthful appearance. During sleep, the body repairs itself, and the brain processes information and emotions. Lack of sleep can lead to a weakened immune system, decreased cognitive function, and increased stress levels.

Tip: Establish a regular sleep routine by going to bed and waking up at the same time each day. Create a restful environment by minimizing noise, reducing screen time before bed, and ensuring our bedroom is dark and comfortable.

Incorporating these eight health secrets into your daily routine can transform your approach to wellness, ensuring that you stay healthy and vibrant at any age. By prioritizing emotional, spiritual, and mental health, you'll find yourself not just living longer, but living better, with high energy and a youthful spirit. Remember, true health is about finding harmony within yourself and the world around you. Embrace this holistic approach to wellness and watch how it enriches every aspect of your life.

Ready to take the next step in your wellness journey? I'm here to help you achieve lasting transformation and vibrant health. Whether you need personalized coaching, want to join a supportive community, or seek guidance in refining your wellness strategies, I'm just a message away.

Contact me at or visit my website [your website URL] to learn more about how we can work together. Let's embark on this journey towards ageless living and boundless energy together!

About Wynita Walther:

Wynita Walther is a writer, teacher and coach for ambitious women. As a former Communications Director from Chicago, Wynita now resides in the hill country of Texas, teaching clients how to live healthy, successful lives, full of faith and aligned with God. Sign up for free and easy to apply weekly faith tips, on her website wynita.com.

Instagram: @queenwynita

# About Wynita Walther

Wynita Walther is a writer, teacher and coach for ambitious women. As a former Communications Director from Chicago, Wynita now resides in the hill country of Texas, teaching clients how to live healthy, successful lives, full of faith and aligned with God. Sign up for free and easy to apply weekly faith tips, on her website wynita.com.

Contact me on Instagram queenwynita or visit my website www.wynita.com to learn more about how we can work together. Let's embark on this journey towards ageless living and boundless energy together!

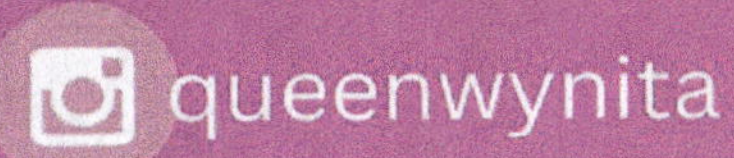


www.wynita.com

# Renee Brown

## CEO/Founder of Renee's Refine & Refresh Travels

I am a Travel Business Owner for almost 2 years now, and I enjoy every minute of it. I am a mother of 2 daughters, and a granddaughter. I enjoy taking family vacations with my girls making family memories together to cherish for a lifetime.

I have always loved to travel and I have found a way where I can save and travel more! I provide services related to travel from one location to another, because travel makes you modest.

The great glory of travel to me is not just what I see that is new to me in places visited but that in almost every one of them I change from an outsider looking in to an insider looking out.

I am a Travelpreneur and I love what I do!

## SUMMER TRAVEL:

Travel is the sexiest industry in the world and people are traveling more everyday...especially during the summertime!

From solo travelers to big groups, whatever your total count of travelers is, you are sure to have a blast. Summer is the most highly rated time of the year to travel, and families are taking the kids to beautiful destination all around the world. Making Memories and enjoying life!

There a numerous places to visit during the summer with your family, and the most popular one is Disney World, right! Who does not want to spend time with Mickey and Friends? Disney is so magical that your family will remember it for a lifetime. They have various parks from Magic Kingdom, EPCOT, Hollywood Studios, Animal Kingdom, and Theme Park. Whatever you choose to do, you are sure to have a BLAST!

## DESTINATIONS:

Looking for a great place to take your family on vacation this summer? Parents are taking the family on exotic places like Bahamas, Jamaica, The Caribbean's, Cruises, Dominican Republic, Japan, Australia, you name it from A to Z. Families are exploring more with the kiddos during the summer, because this is the best time that school is out the longest to travel.

Parents also enjoy taking their kids to these place to see other parts of the world. They get to be educated on the various cultures and have fun doing it.

There are also the beaches where you can soak up the sun, ride the waves, or just lay by the shore.

Kayaking on sparkling bays, hike to see waterfalls in a rainforest, take tours of the islands, and enjoy all the different foods at each destination. Your mouth will truly have a vacation of its own as well, which offer all-inclusive at various resorts so you can experience it all without missing a beat.

Take the family on a tour, which are guided by professional tour guides throughout your stay.

Vacations give families the opportunity to explore together, and they provide the backdrop for shared memories between parents and their kids. Which cultivates closer family bond. Vacationing as a family can also a relieve stress, by helping teach children to adapt to new situations, build their confidence and give them a broader perspective on the world.

Summer vacation gives you a chance to hang out and appreciate one another, so rather you are building sandcastles or enjoying meal in another country it will be a hit amongst everyone there. So don't be afraid to explore the world and see it one place at a time. Take the vacation that you and your family both deserves, The BEST summer getaways are planned TOGETHER and where everyone will sure to be pleased!

So whatever your choice is for your family during the summer time, make it memorable and fun. Your kids are not going to stay young for long, so get out there and enjoy life!!!

# TRAVEL AGENT SUGGESTS

## The Best
## Family Vacation Spots
### for 2024

From laid-back islands to charming small towns and bustling cities, here are some of the best family summer vacation ideas...

## Local destinations:

- Orlando
- Wisconsin Dells
- Gatlinburg
- Washington, D.C
- Myrtle Beach
- Cape Cod
- Yosemite National Park
- Grand Canyon National Park

## International destinations:

- Europe
- Greece
- Italy
- France
- Puerto Rico
- Japan

Pictures Ahead!

Walt Disney World

Universal Studios-
Orlando, Florida
Resort and Theme Park

Washington DC-
United States Capitol

Washington DC-
United States Capitol

Lake Como-
Italy

Japan and China-
Cultural Discovery

# FOCUS

# SPOTLIGHT GUEST ANTONY CARTER AKA ANTONE

## FROM CHICAGO ILLINOIS

Antony is a product of the south side of Chicago. He grew up in church singing in an A Cappella worship environment where the emphasis was on tight harmonious singing. His father was the choir director and worship leader. Antony took piano lessons from the age of five and soon began to play the trumpet, drums, and saxophone. In high school he expanded into writing, recording, and producing his own music as well as joining his first band and although music videos were brand new in the industry, Antony even directed and shot a music video of one of his original songs.

From high school until now Antony has continued performing, writing, producing, and recording music in multiple genres. He has been featured on hundreds of festivals,corporate, wedding and church stages in Chicago and the Midwest. Antony is the lead singer for two live performance bands - the Associates Band and Second City Soul. He has flourished as a solo Neo Soul artist under the pseudonym, Antone, having written, produced, and released 2 R&B CD's and many singles. Several of the songs off these projects have been featured on internet radio and have been made into music videos. "She Knows" by Antone is his R&B hit song that is rising in popularity quickly around the world on streaming platforms. Search Antone She Knows on any music streaming platform and enjoy! You can thank me later. Antony has also stayed connected to his gospel roots. For over 20 years he was choir director and worship leader for his church, and member of a traveling gospel Quintet – The United Quintet of Chicago. !

As director of his church choir Antony recorded 7 CD's and won a Christian Acapella Music Award in 2004. He also released his solo gospel recording entitled, "My All". Antony is most proud of the gospel songs he has been inspired with that have touched countless lives. He is the songwriter of "If Anybody Has A Reason To Sing & quot;, " Sweet Peace of Mind", and "Give Me A Song To Sing, Like Jesus& quot;. These songs have been sung in worship services each Sunday around the country for many years touching hearts and lives. To God be the glory

# MUSIC & ENTERTAINMENT

## SUN ENSEMBLE JAZZ BAND

## SUN ENSEMBLE

Established 1984, Chicago, IL 60619
Follow us on FACEBOOK

This fabulous band has been performing in Chicago and the Chicago area for over 50 years. We have also had occasion to play to audiences in other cities around the world .

My name is Tazama Sun, founder of the Sun Ensemble jazz band.

This is a story about my band, and my journey to become an accomplished musician.

I started playing my first instrument at the age of 6. I would practice for many hours a day for seemingly months, until one day while playing my violin it became fun. I studied and practiced every day until I was a professional violinist. I played for church, school, and entertainment spots in my hometown.
As a teenager I came to Chicago and enchanted my talents at Chicago State University music program. While there I studied under several professors and band instructors. I joined many school bands playing jazz,blues, rock,soul,and pop music. By this time I started exclusively playing the saxophone. I mastered techniques of fine tune playing of the alto,soprano, tenor,and bass saxophones.

I developed friendships with many musicians. Some of whom now have notable careers on worldwide stages, movies, and other major productions. I have held on to many friendships throughout the years. Which allowed me to become active in several professional bands and theatrical productions while still a student and years many after.

I founded my band Sun Ensemble in 1984 upon my graduation from Chicago State University. And after having success in the business of entertainment. Through the years we have employed many different musicians, who have rotated in and out of bands for various reasons. Most of our former band members are still, to this day, my cherished friends.

Currently Sun Ensemble is composed of seven fantastic outstanding musicians who are very accomplished in a variety of musical styles. We play jazz, pop,top 40s, blues, soul,and fusion.

Sun Ensemble has performed in most of the top clubs and theaters in Chicago, Indiana, and Wisconsin. In 1984 we were booked at 3 clubs or more each week. Clubs like Eves in the south suburban area where we were the house band for 3 years. We've been booked at many of the City of Chicago summer events, Lee's Unleaded Blues Club on 74th and South Chicago, The Dating Game on 88th and Stony Island. For over the last 10 years we have been performing one Saturday each month at Chant restaurant in Hyde Park, Chicago.

The Sun Ensemble is a group of musicians that are dedicated to creativeness, Jazz blues,R&B, Dance, Rock and the listeners of music that will transit the world.

Explore
the World
on your terms
BUILD A NETWORK
EMPOWER YOURSELF AND OTHERS
GAIN
Financial FREEDOM
Personal FREEDOM
Time FREEDOM
R&N WRIGHT GLOBAL
TRAVEL CONCIERGE
PlanNet
MARKETING

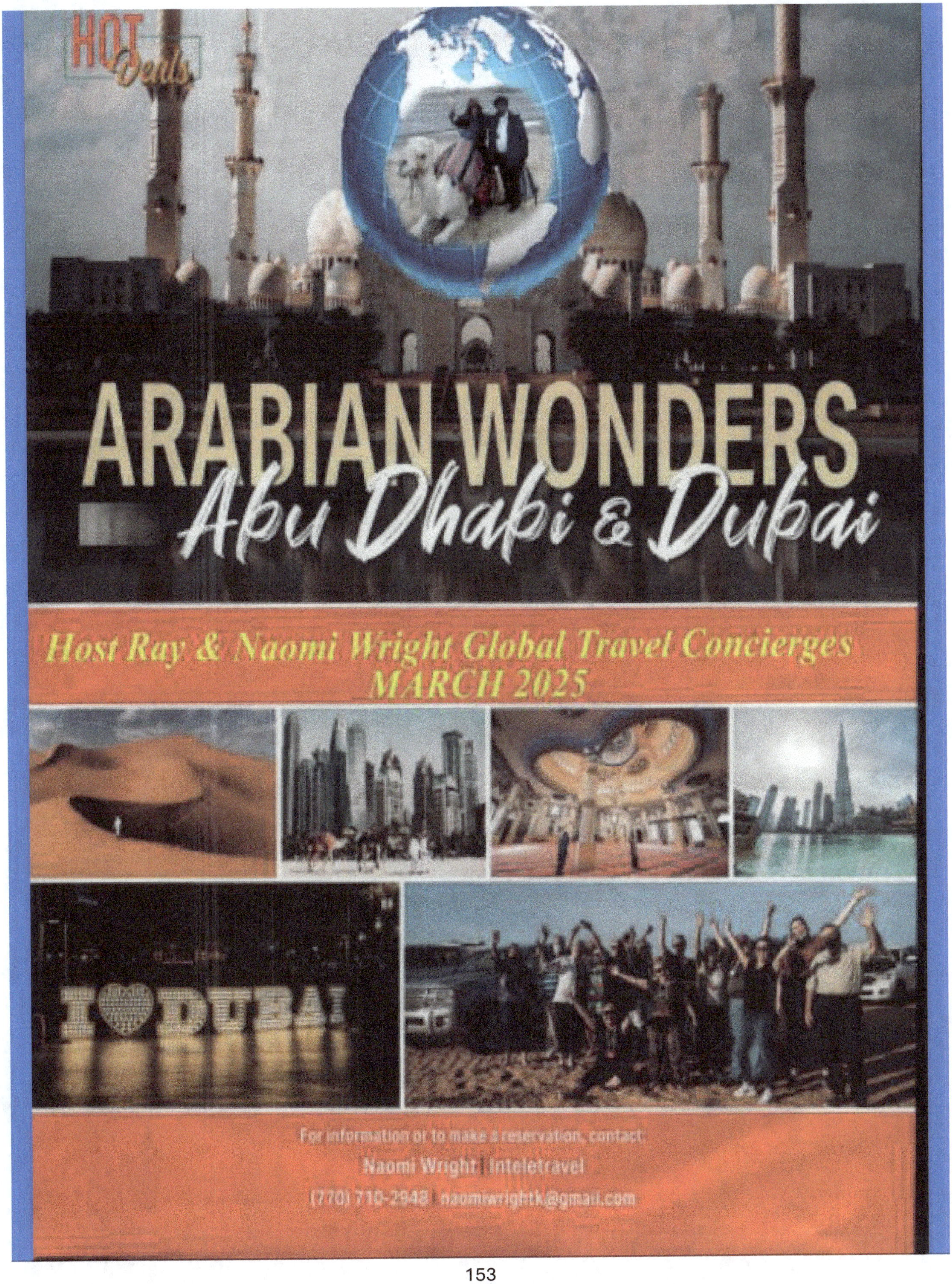

# ARABIAN WONDERS
## Abu Dhabi & Dubai



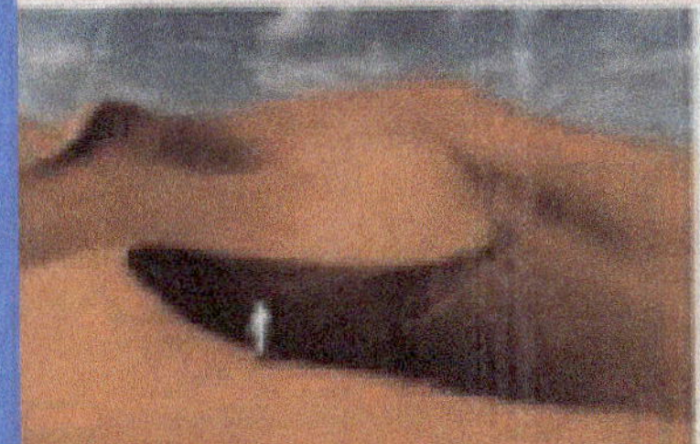

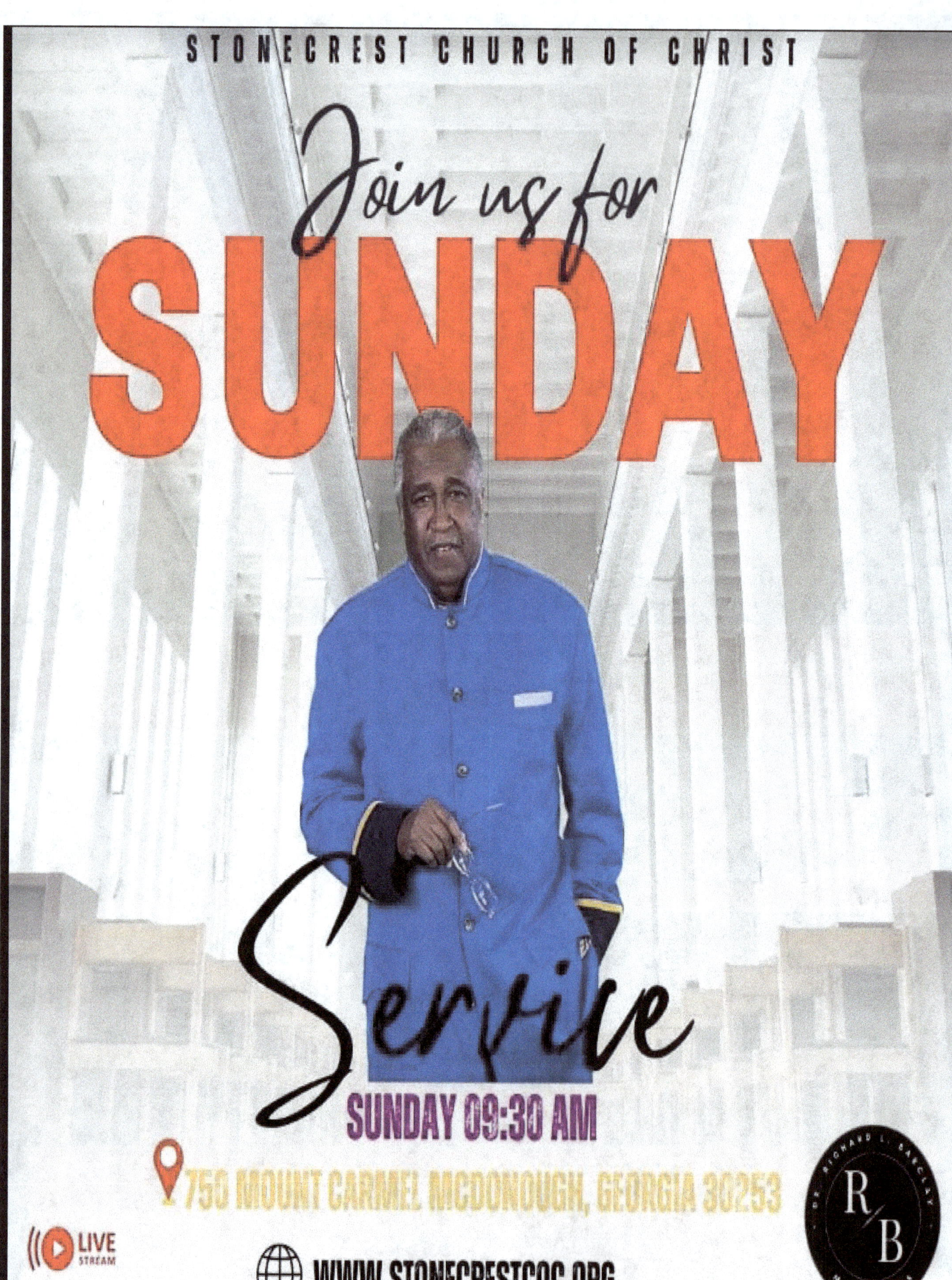
STONECREST CHURCH OF CHRIST
Join us for
SUNDAY
Service
SUNDAY 09:30 AM
750 MOUNT CARMEL MCDONOUGH, GEORGIA 30253
LIVE STREAM
WWW.STONECRESTCOC.ORG
DR. RICHARD L. BARCLAY MINISTRIES
R/B

# STONECREST CHURCH OF CHRIST
## PRESENTS

**12-13TH OCTOBER 2024**

DR. RICHARD L BARCLAY
HOST MINISTER

BROTHER PAUL WILLIAMS
GUEST SONG LEADER

BROTHER WESLEY LEONARD
GUEST MINISTER

**Saturday 10/12/24**
**5 pm**
**Songfest**

**Sunday 10/13/24**
**9:30 am**
**Worship**

750 Mt. Carmel Rd, McDonough, GA 30253
404-474-1908
www.stonecrestcoc.org

# Lorena Douglas

Lorena Woods Douglas leverages more than 30 years of professional experience as an expert in the field of marketing. Since 2017, she has served as the chief executive officer of The MITA Agency, and since 2011, she has held the same role at Mobile Marketing Branding Solutions in Atlanta, Georgia. A proven leader in her profession, Mrs. Douglas specializes in digital marketing, and over the course of her career, she has excelled as an entrepreneur, assisting other business owners with various marketing management needs.

Adjacent to her primary vocational endeavors, Ms. Douglas has also served as the owner of Lorena's Day Spa since 1982. Featured in National Magazine (Nail Pro Magazine) in 1995. She served on the Archer Daniel Midland Bargaining Committee 8 years, Decatur Chambers Of Commerce, Furthermore, she has hosted her own radio podcast, "Destiny Driven Radio, " since 2011. In her other creative endeavors, she authored the 214 book, "Finding Your Passion in Life and Discovery Your Destiny in the Process." Featured in Amazing Women Magazine April 2015 Well-regarded for her accomplishments, Mrs. Douglas has been honored with several accolades, including receiving the President Barack Obama The Presidential Lifetime Achievement Award 2017, and Mayor Award for Achievement as a Business owner 19. In light of her fulfilling career, she largely attributes her success to her drive and determination.

SHOP NOW FOR
STYLISH STATEMENTS

Visit giselemonique.com to explore our full collection and find the perfect gear to showcase your dedication to the medical field. Elevate your wardrobe and express your passion with Gisele Monique!

IT'S NOT THE
SI7E
Of The
NEEDLE
IT'S THE SKILL OF THE
PHLEBOTOMIST
!!!

ELEVATE YOUR
MEDICAL WARDROBE
WITH OUR UNIQUE
T-SHIRT QUOTES!
SHOP NOW - WWW.GISELEMONIQUE.COM

GISELEMONIQUE.COM

## Atlanta Caribbean Carnival : Impulz Xperience Mas Band Brings Excellence to Atlanta

Nestled in the vibrant city of Stonecrest, Georgia, **Impulz Xperience** Mas Band has emerged as a beacon of Caribbean culture, infusing the spirit of Trinidad and Tobago's legendary carnival into the heart of Atlanta. Spearheaded by the dynamic Keisha Simon, a Trinidadian native with deep roots in Brooklyn, New York, this mas band is redefining the local festival scene with its elegant and authentic flair.

Keisha Simon, the driving force behind Impulz Xperience, embodies the multicultural journey that has shaped her life. Born in Trinidad, she moved to Brooklyn at a young age, where the vibrant Caribbean community and its lively traditions left an indelible mark on her. For the past 25 years, Atlanta has been her home, a city where she has raised her three children. Her life
story is a testament to the rich tapestry of Caribbean-American culture, blending heritage with modernity.

The inception of Impulz Xperience Mas Band was sparked by a simple yet powerful idea: to bring the exuberance and elegance of Trinidad and Tobago's carnival to Atlanta. It all began with Keisha and her three close friends, united by a shared passion for their cultural roots and a desire to showcase the vibrancy of carnival with a touch of sophistication. Their vision was clear—to create a mas band that not only celebrated Caribbean traditions but did so with a unique twist, one that exuded elegance and grace.

This year marked a significant milestone for Impulz Xperience as they made their debut at the Atlanta Caribbean Carnival. The excitement was palpable as the band took to the streets, dazzling onlookers with their stunning costumes, infectious energy, and the rhythmic beats of Soca music. It was a moment of pride for Keisha and her team, a culmination of months of hard work, creativity, and dedication.

The theme of their inaugural presentation was a homage to the beauty and diversity of the Caribbean. Lavish feathers, vibrant colors, and intricate designs adorned the costumes, each one telling a story of its own.

From the regal purple and gold ensembles symbolizing the ocean and the sun to the fiery reds and oranges representing the island sunsets, every costume was a masterpiece, crafted with meticulous attention to detail.

But Impulz Xperience is more than just a mas band; it's a community, a family. Keisha's vision extends beyond the carnival stage. She is passionate about fostering a sense of belonging and pride among Caribbean-Americans in Atlanta, providing a platform for cultural expression and connection. The band's activities go beyond the parade, including community outreach, cultural workshops, and events that celebrate Caribbean heritage throughout the year.

The debut at the Atlanta Caribbean Carnival is just the beginning for Impulz Xperience. Keisha and her team have big plans for the future. They aim to become a staple in the Atlanta festival circuit, growing their band, and continuing to innovate and inspire. The dream is to create an annual spectacle that draws participants and spectators from all over, making Atlanta a key destination for carnival enthusiasts.

For Keisha, the journey is personal and profound. It's about honoring her roots, sharing her culture with her children, and building a legacy that bridges the gap between the Caribbean and the United States. Her story, and that of Impulz Xperience, is a celebration of resilience, creativity, and the unbreakable spirit of the Caribbean diaspora. Her goal, mission, and vision will always be to uplift her community, preserve her heritage, and inspire future generations to embrace and celebrate their cultural identity.

As the sounds of Soca music fade into the warm Atlanta night and the last feathers are packed away, one thing is clear: Impulz Xperience Mas Band has made its mark. With elegance, passion, and an unwavering commitment to cultural authenticity, they have brought a piece of the Caribbean to Atlanta, and they are here to stay. The future of Atlanta's carnival scene is brighter and more vibrant with Impulz Xperience leading the way, promising many more years of joy, dance, and celebration.

# Impulz Xperience –

## Feel the Vibes, Experience the Mas.

www.impulzxperience.com

YUNG GOTTI
"GO OVERTIME TO INVENT" = G.O.T.T.I


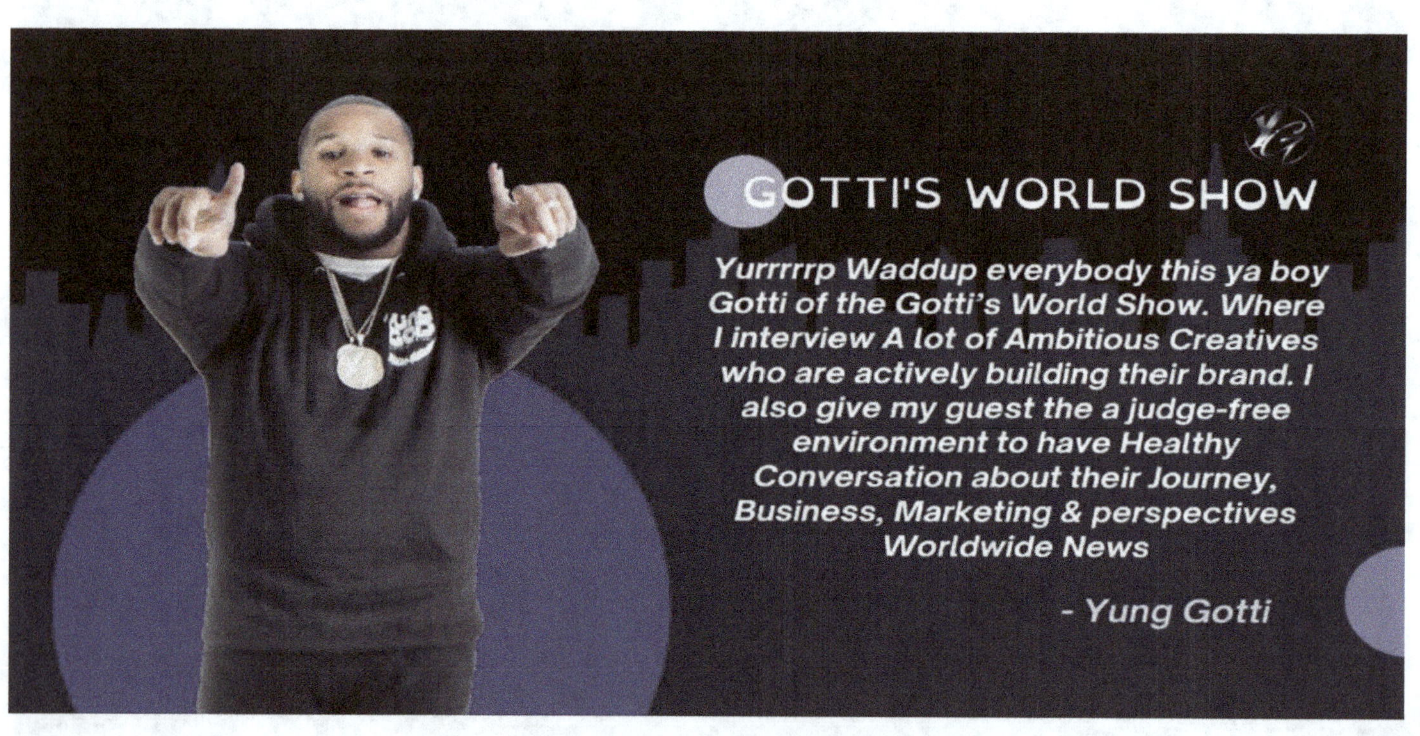

GOTTI'S WORLD SHOW
Yurrrrrp Waddup everybody this ya boy Gotti of the Gotti's World Show. Where I interview A lot of Ambitious Creatives who are actively building their brand. I also give my guest the a judge-free environment to have Healthy Conversation about their Journey, Business, Marketing & perspectives Worldwide News
- Yung Gotti

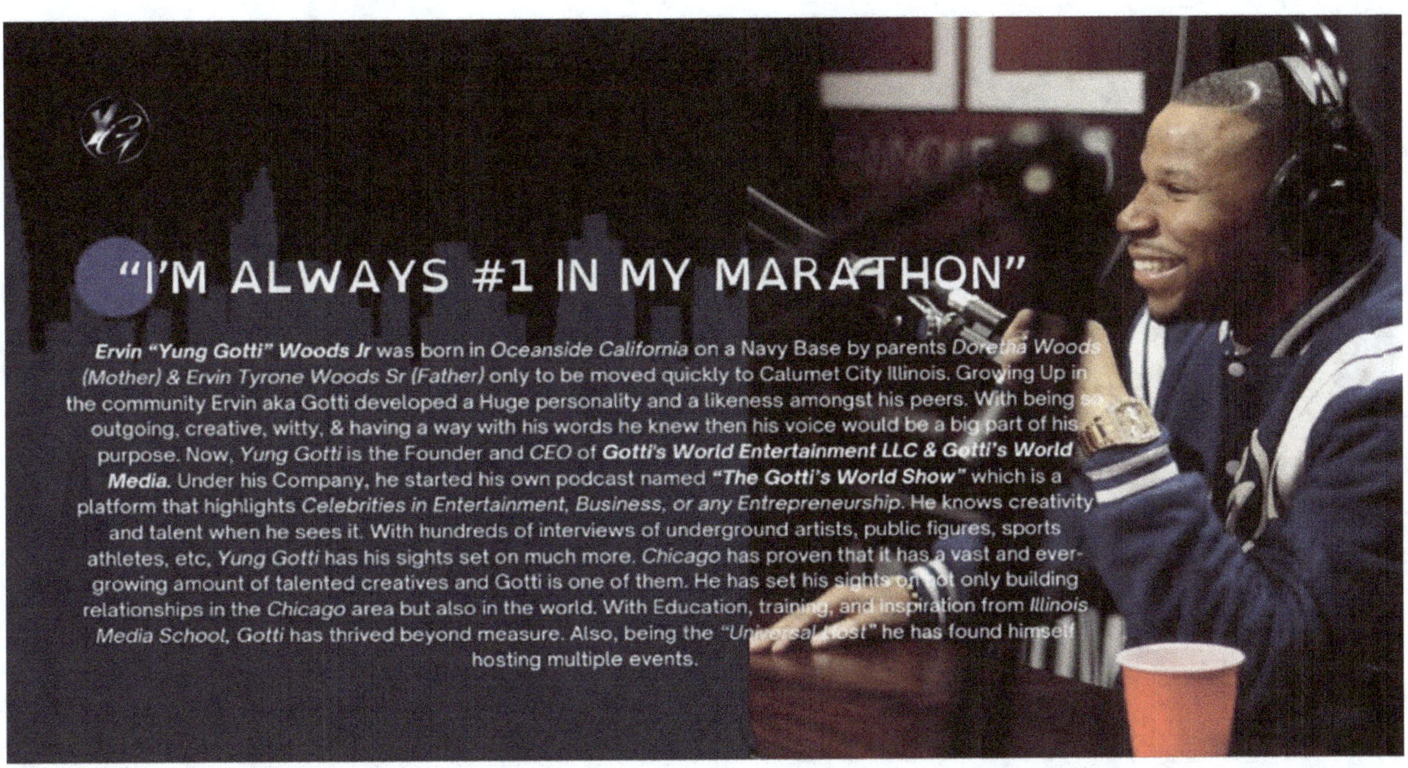



Ervin *"Yung Gotti" Woods Jr* was born in *Oceanside California* on a Navy Base by parents *Doretha Woods (Mother)* & *Ervin Tyrone Woods Sr (Father)* only to be moved quickly to Calumet City Illinois. Growing Up in the community Ervin aka Gotti developed a Huge personality and a likeness amongst his peers. With being so outgoing, creative, witty, & having a way with his words he knew then his voice would be a big part of his purpose. Now, *Yung Gotti* is the Founder and *CEO* of *Gotti's World Entertainment LLC & Gotti's World Media*. Under his Company, he started his own podcast named *"The Gotti's World Show"* which is a platform that highlights *Celebrities in Entertainment, Business, or any Entrepreneurship*. He knows creativity and talent when he sees it. With hundreds of interviews of underground artists, public figures, sports athletes, etc, *Yung Gotti* has his sights set on much more. *Chicago* has proven that it has a vast and ever-growing amount of talented creatives and Gotti is one of them. He has set his sights on not only building relationships in the *Chicago* area but also in the world. With Education, training, and inspiration from *Illinois Media School, Gotti* has thrived beyond measure. Also, being the *"Universal Host"* he has found himself hosting multiple events.

GOTTI'S WORLD SHOW

PROFESSIONAL HOST
Host for Live Concerts, Podcasts, Radio, Television, Theater, Weddings, Guest Speaker, Night Club Host, Youth Events, Talent Shows, Showcase Host, Conference Host / Speaker, Birthday Host, and In Gotti's words " I never chose podcasting but Podcasting chose me." Gotti clarifies this statement by saying it is because it related to everything he already was.. No guidelines, Structure, just open conversations with creative personalities.

EVENT RECAP PREVIEW
Host - Wild Hare Wednesday Artist Showcase - 4/2022
Host - Chicago Unity Event - 6/2022
Host - Icon Anniversary Bowling Event- 2/2022
Guest Judge - Poetry Slam Event- 2/2022
Guest Judge - Drakes Youth Apollo Night- 4/2022
Special Guest Speaker - Entertainment Class - 4/2022
Special Guest judge with Rich Homie Quan - 5/2022 more...

GALLERY

GOTTI
GO LIVE
INSTAGRAM LIVE
HOSTED BY
YUNG GOTTI
@official_yunggotti
708-297-7753
Ewoodsjr023gmail.com
linktr.ee/GOTTIWORLDMEDIA
GOTTI'S WORLD, GLOBAL
"GOTTI GO LIVE" ON INSTAGRAM
LIVE EVERY THURSDAY 8PM
"LEAD WITH LOVE & MOTIVATION"

# Plant God's Seed Presents
## Meh'thik Aroma

מֶתֶק אֲרוֹמָה

Plant God's Seed is a faith-based business selling Luxurious Unisex Roll-On Perfumes called Meh'thik Aroma that stems from The Song of Solomon 1:3. The CEO and Creative Director Breana Anjàe curated a product after her baptism with the help of the Holy Spirit to always let her worship rise like a sweet perfume.
Orders can be made at : **www.PlantGodsSeed.com**
Contact us at: **anjaebplanttheseed@gmail.com**
**Instagram: breanaanjae_**
**PlantGodsseed_**

**Blossom with fragrances:**

**KINGDDOM RAIDIANCE**
Uni-sex frankincense, arabian oud, and authority

**REMNANT**
indian musk, frankincense, and a chosen nation

**BELOVED HEIR**
Clean, baby powder scent with a hint of joy

**NOBLE -ESSENCE**
Luxurious and classy with a hint of power.

**SACRED LILY**
Musk and vanilla blend for a sophisticated allure and purity

# Plant God's Seed Presents:

# Meh'thik Aroma
## מֶתֶק אֲרוֹמָה

Plant God's Seed is a faith-based business selling Luxurious Unisex Roll-On Perfumes called Meh'thik Aroma that stems from Songs of Solomon 1:3. The CEO and Creative Director Breana Anjàe curated a product after her baptism with the help of the Holy Spirit to always let her worship rise like a sweet perfume. Orders can be made at : www.PlantGodsSeed.com

## Blossom with fragrances:

### KINGDDOM RAIDIANCE
Uni-sex frankincense, arabian oud, and authority

### REMNANT
indian musk, frankincense, and a chosen nation

### BELOVED HEIR
Clean, baby powder scent with a hint of joy

### NOBLE -ESSENCE
Luxurious and classy with a hint of power.

### SACRED LILY
Musk and vanilla blend for a sophisticated allure and purity

# DENNIS DANTZLER SR

## THE REACTION BAND: METRO ATLANTA'S PREMIER PERFORMERS FOR EVERY OCCASION

The reaction band was started by Dennis Dantzler, who is a guitarist, singer and songwriter The musicians were chosen based on their musical versatility, and their great past experiences.

The band is very versatile and able to take on any event. A successful, fun and enjoying event is always guaranteed. With a repertoire that spans genres and decades, The Reaction Band masterfully blends classic hits with contemporary favorites, ensuring that every guest finds something to enjoy. Their dynamic stage presence and exceptional musicianship have earned them a reputation as the go-to band for those looking to elevate their event to the next level.

Each member of The Reaction Band brings their own unique talent and flair to the group, creating a synergy that makes their performances truly unforgettable. Whether they're covering soulful ballads, funky grooves, or chart-topping pop songs, The Reaction Band's passion for music shines through, making every show a celebration.

For any occasion, please call 404-418-4125 to book The Reaction Band and ensure your event is a success. When it comes to live entertainment, they are the perfect choice for any event where only the best will do.

# SHINING IN HIS ROLE

# THE REACTION BAND

## Metro Atlanta's Premier Performers for Every Occasion

**For any occasion, reach out at 404-418-4125 or 678-361-2642.**